KU-997-450

STUDIES IN CHRISTIAN WORSHIP 8

The Feast of Pentecost

WITHDRAWN
FROM STOCK

By the same author:

THE LITURGY OF PENANCE

The Feast of Pentecost

The Great Fifty Days in the Liturgy

By JOHN GUNSTONE

THE FAITH PRESS
7 Tufton Street, London, S.W.1

FIRST PUBLISHED IN 1967

© *John Gunstone, 1967*

PRINTED IN GREAT BRITAIN
in 10 point Times Roman
BY THE FAITH PRESS LTD.
LEIGHTON BUZZARD

To
G. W. O. Addleshaw

Contents

Preface

The significance of the great Fifty Days between Easter Day and Whitsunday is often overlooked in the Church's teaching and worship. In writing about the Christian year, scholars are more attracted by the drama of Holy Week, especially since the revisions to the Roman rite in 1955; clergy and congregations are usually so absorbed in their Lenten projects that they forget the great season for which Lent is but a preparation.

An attempt to recover the status of the great Fifty Days in the calendar is not just liturgical purism. It is a matter that is very relevant to our pastoral teaching. We are learning that the ministry of the Word at the eucharist is as important as the ministry of the Sacrament. Before the faithful approach the Lord's Table, passages of scripture are read, culminating in the proclamation of the gospel, to invoke their sense of thanksgiving for their redemption in Christ; and to proclaim the Easter event, without realizing the fulfilment of hope symbolized by the seven weeks that follow, is to cut short the meaning of that redemption.

This essay is a brief excursion into a select area of liturgical theology: it attempts to trace the effect movements of thought and custom have had over the centuries on the way the Church ministered the Word of God. We shall see how the great Fifty Days rose in their primitive unity and then were fragmented into the collection of vigils, festivals, octaves and fasts which now appear in the Roman missal and in the Book of Common Prayer and its successors.

Unlike Lent or Holy Week, the great Fifty Days have no visual aids to teach the congregation the meaning of the mysteries they celebrate. There are no ashes or palm branches. (I discount local customs, such as the scattering of roses from the hole in the dome of the Pantheon in Rome during the stational mass on the Sunday after Ascension Day, or the 'Whit walk' in the north of England!) Everything depends on the choice of readings, on the way the readings are expounded in the sermon, and on the chants or hymns selected to express the congregation's response to the Word.

The revision of the lectionary concerns both Anglicans and

9

Roman Catholics to-day (could it be a joint concern?). In this book I have tried to sketch in the background for such a revision in the period between Easter and Whitsun, the crown of the liturgical year. In order to do so, I have had to probe into patristic and liturgical texts along ways marked out by many scholars. The footnotes indicate only a little how much I have depended upon them.

I am particularly grateful to the Rev. John A. Ponter, a colleague from a neighbouring parish, who helped me with the translations of some passages from the Cappadocian Fathers. If there are errors, they are mine, not his.

It so happened that the manuscript was being corrected during the season which is the subject of the essay. As a result, I found my own understanding of and participation in the liturgy of the great Fifty Days enormously enriched by the works of our forefathers in the faith. The 'week of weeks' came alive for me in a vivid and inspiring way. If it helps others to share in a similar experience, then it will have been even more worthwhile.

Saturday in the Octave of Pentecost, 1966

I. *The Feast of Weeks*

In New Testament times the three principal festivals of the Jews were the feast of Passover-Unleavened Bread, the feast of Weeks, and the feast of Tabernacles. Although there were other public and private observances, these three stand out in the calendar as occasions when the people went up to Jerusalem to join in the celebrations at the temple. Some of the psalms echo the mood of those pilgrimage processions:

> 'I was glad when they said unto me:
>   We will go into the house of the Lord.
> Our feet shall stand in thy gates:
>   O Jerusalem.' [1]

Jews dispersed throughout the Mediterranean countries used the festivals as opportunities for visiting the holy city, so that it was quite likely one would meet there on such an occasion 'Parthians, Medes, Elamites; inhabitants of Mesopotamia, of Judaea and Cappadocia, of Pontus and Asia, of Phrygia and Pamphylia, of Egypt and the districts of Libya around Cyrene; visitors from Rome, both Jews and proselytes, Cretans and Arabs.' [2]

All three festivals seem to have originated among the early Israelites in religious cults of a pastoral and agricultural kind. The ritual of Passover suggests that it began as a springtime sacrifice for fertility and prosperity among nomadic or semi-nomadic folk. No other Israelite observance is more like the sacrifices of the ancient Arabs. Its characteristics were a lamb roasted over an open fire without the use of kitchen utensils, the eating of the victim with unleavened bread and bitter herbs (desert plants), and the custom that the participants should be dressed as for a journey with their belts fastened and sandals on their feet. Particularly primitive features were

[1] Exod. 23:17; 34:23; Psalm 122:1–2.
[2] Acts 2:8–11.

11

the use of blood and the absence of any temple, altar or formal priesthood.

In contrast, the rites connected with Unleavened Bread indicate its beginnings in a more settled community with time to sow and reap. The feast marked the opening of the barley harvest, the first of the corn crops to be gathered. The purpose of the festival was to offer to God the firstfruits of the first harvest. 'When you come into the land which I give you and reap its harvest, you shall bring the sheaf of the firstfruits of your harvest to the priest; and he shall wave the sheaf before the Lord that you may find acceptance; on the morrow after the sabbath the priest shall wave it.'[3] During the first seven days, only bread made from the newly reaped grain was eaten; it did not contain any leaven from the harvest of the previous year.

It is not known how Unleavened Bread came to be associated with Passover. Deuteronomy and the reform of Josiah made Passover, like Unleavened Bread, a pilgrimage feast, so the two may have been brought together before the exile. The fact that both were springtime observances and that they both used unleavened bread may also have had something to do with it. Whatever the reason, by our Lord's time Passover was kept on the day before Unleavened Bread. St. Mark calls the two-day observance 'the festival of Passover and Unleavened Bread' and St. Luke refers to 'Unleavened Bread, known as Passover.' Josephus tells his readers that it was celebrated by the Jews 'with sacrifices on a vast scale.'[4]

The dates for the feast were calculated each year by the phases of the moon, but the method of doing this was a matter of dispute between the Pharisees and the Boethuseans, a party among the Sadducees. The differences arose out of the interpretation of the 'morrow after the sabbath' laid down in the Levitical code. In the end the Pharisee's method of fixing Passover on the fourteenth day of the first month, *Nisan* (March–April), Unleavened Bread on the fifteenth day (and treating it as the sabbath referred to in Leviticus), and the Sheaf-waving in the temple on the sixteenth day was eventually followed in Jerusalem. Although there is some evidence that the festival was still kept in the home (was the last supper a Passover meal?) it had come to be centred on the ritual in the temple.

[3] Leviticus 23:10–11.
[4] *The Jewish War*, ed. G. A. Williamson (Penguin Classics), p. 114.

12

The feast of Unleavened Bread looked forward to the completion of the grain harvest which was celebrated on the second of the three pilgrimage festivals, the feast of Weeks. A period of fifty days—a 'week' of weeks—was reckoned 'from the moment when the sickle begins to cut the grain.' [5] This was computed from the day of the Sheaf-waving. These seven weeks had a special significance because it was believed that God, who gave the former and the latter rain, reserved this period for the purpose of harvesting.

In some parts of the Old Testament the festival is called the feast of Firstfruits. Its Aramaic title, *Asarta,* implied the conclusion of an observance and a reunion of the people. The rabbis referred to it as the 'closing assembly of the Passover.' However, it was the number of days separating the feast of Weeks from the feast of Passover-Unleavened Bread which gave it a distinctive name among Greek-speaking Jews— *Pentecost,* Fifty.

The Greek title first appears in the Apocrypha, where the book of Tobit mentions 'the feast of Pentecost, which is the holy feast of the seven weeks.' [6] The ceremonies connected with it included an offering of two loaves made out of the new flour from that year's harvest and baked with leaven. This is the only instance in which the use of yeast is prescribed for a ritual offering (leaven was regarded as ceremonially impure). On the first day of the wheat harvest unleavened bread was eaten as a sign of a new beginning; on the last day leavened bread was offered because this was the ordinary bread of the farming community and the feast symbolized a return to normal customs. According to the Old Testament it was kept as early as the reign of Solomon. [7]

The feast of Tabernacles has a more obscure origin. It marked the end of the whole harvesting season, when the produce of vineyards and orchards had been gathered in— another name for it was the feast of Ingathering. It tended to be the most crowded of all the festivals. The feast began on the fifteenth day of the seventh month, *Tishri* (September– October) and continued for seven days. It was a time of merrymaking, when even the respected members of the community joined in the dances in the temple courtyard, singing

[5] Deuteronomy 16:9.
[6] Tobit 2:1. Also 2 Maccabees 12:31–2.
[7] 1 Kings 9:25. J. B. Segal, *The Hebrew Passover,* p. 180.

and brandishing torches with what Isaiah calls 'joy in harvest.' The name of the celebration may have been derived from the tents or huts which were (and still are) erected in Judah in the vineyards and orchards while the grapes and fruit were gathered.[8]

At different times both the feast of Passover and the feast of Weeks came to be associated with major events in the salvation-history of Israel. In this process, the old pastoral and agricultural themes were not lost, but interwoven with them was a profound sense of awe and thankfulness for all that God had done for his people. Throughout the centuries priest and prophet, psalmist and chronicler constantly reminded Israel of God's mighty work, so it is not surprising that in time the saving events came to be celebrated within the context of existing festivals.

The association of the feast of Passover with the exodus from Egypt and the crossing of the Red Sea is very early indeed—so early that details of the festival are interwoven into the account of the exodus in the Old Testament itself. Scholars believe that this is the work of the P source in the Pentateuch.[9] Its theme is that the ritual of the feast was instituted by God both to assist in the escape from Egypt and to provide a means of commemorating the liberation year by year. We can say, therefore, that four or five hundred years before Christ, the feast of Passover meant to the Israelites a celebration of the exodus as well as the offering of the first of the grain harvest. Passover means 'passage,' and the passage through the Red Sea became to Judaism what the life, death and resurrection of Jesus Christ are to the New Testament and the Church.[10]

In a similar way Pentecost came to be regarded as a com-

[8] J. Pedersen, *Israel: its Life and Culture,* vols. iii–iv, pp. 401ff., and R. de Vaux, *Ancient Israel: its Life and Institutions,* pp. 484ff.

[9] J, E and P are among the familiar symbols used in commentaries to denote the different traditions behind these books of the Old Testament. The J source has been identified because, among other things, it uses the form *Yahweh* (*Jahweh*) for the name of God; the E source uses *Elohim*. Both these sources are believed to be pre-exilic, perhaps preserving traditions from the southern and northern kingdoms respectively. The P symbol is used to label material which, because of its content and character, seems to have originated among post-exilic circles in Jerusalem.

[10] The significance of this is discussed in another book in the present series, *The Sacrament of Easter* by Roger Greenacre.

memoration of the giving of the Law on Sinai, but this was not until many centuries after the association of the Exodus with Passover. No hint of the association appears in the Old Testament texts. The P source may have been responsible for attributing the event to 'the third moon after the people of Israel had gone forth out of the land of Egypt'—an interval which could be interpreted as one of fifty days—but it does not seem to have been the intention to link the theophany on the mount with the feast of Weeks.

The main events connected with the Law-giving are in Exodus 19 to 24. Basically the text is a conflation of two accounts, one from J and the other from E, but it has been so worked over and glosses added that it is almost impossible to disentangle the original sources. There is the story of Moses summoned up the mountain and the description of the thunders and lightnings and thick cloud, the trumpet and the voice of God. Directions for purification and for the offering of sacrifice are intermingled with references to Aaron, Aaron's sons, the elders and the young men. But the core of the event is the spelling out of the decalogue and the ordinances of the law in the following chapters. The whole collection made up the 'Book of the Covenant' to be accepted by the people and to be ratified by their leader.

At some time in its transmission, the combined narrative of JE has been edited by a Deuteronomic school of scribes who have given point to the story by stating the purpose of Israel's election:

'Thus shall you say to the house of Jacob, and tell the people of Israel: "You have seen what I did to the Egyptians, and how I bore you on eagles' wings and brought you to myself. Now, therefore, if you will obey my voice and keep my covenant, you shall be my own possession among all peoples; for all the earth is mine, and you shall be to me a kingdom of priests and a holy nation." ' [11]

What bound the people of Israel together as a nation were not the ties of blood or race, but the ties which God had made when he chose them for his own. And the purpose of his choice was that they should be a priestly people in the world, keeping the covenant and being themselves holy. Sinai was a ratification both of their unity and of their vocation.

Reforming movements among the Jews pointed the people

[11] Exodus 19:3–6.

15

back to the covenant on Sinai, and particularly to the purpose of its inauguration, when they recalled the nation to obedience and holiness. Jeremiah and Ezekiel envisaged the establishment of a new covenant which would be enscribed within men's hearts through their unity with the Law-Giver and the Spirit. Later reformers reacted against what they regarded as the corruption of their religion by the priestly circles in Jerusalem and appealed to the Law given on Sinai.

The feast of Weeks became a special symbol for some of these puritan movements. As a commemoration of Sinai, it acted in their eyes as a wholesome corrective and reminder. God had saved his people at the Red Sea—but he had also made a covenant with them. That was the outlook which brought Pentecost to the fore in sectarian Judaism in the period between the Testaments.

It was from this milieu that the *Book of Jubilees* originated. Previously this work had been known only in an Ethiopic and a Latin version and the problem of dating it had not been solved. Now fragments of the book written in Hebrew have been found at Qumran and these indicate that it was composed between 135 and 96 B.C.

The *Book of Jubilees* repeats and develops the stories of Genesis with a timetable based on weeks of years and jubilees, and it gives to the feast of Weeks an importance quite unlike that festival's treatment in the Old Testament. The observance of the feast is assumed in the first sentence of the book. It is the first of the pilgrimage feasts to be prescribed, and it is commanded again and again, always connected with the divine covenants in Israel's history. Passover is not allowed to challenge its prominence: the link between Passover and Pentecost is ignored.

The chronology of the *Book of Jubilees* is so arranged that 'the morrow after the sabbath' laid down in Leviticus is taken to mean the day after the weekly sabbath, and the narrative of the Law-giving is adjusted to show that it occurred on the fifteenth day of the third month. Since Exodus records that Moses was in the mountain for a week after God had commanded him to ascend, the editors of *Jubilees* did some arithmetic and stated that it was seven days before the new moon that Moses was summoned by God: 'The first year of the exodus of the children of Israel, on the third month, the seventh day of the month, God addressed Moses

16

and said to him, "Go before me unto the mountain and I will give you the two tablets of stone of the Law and the precepts." '

A fragmentary liturgical calendar found in cave 4Q at Qumran has made it possible to identify the community's own calendar definitely with that of *Jubilees*.[12] The *Damascus Rule* lays down that the sect's 'Book of the Divisions of the Times into their Jubilees and Weeks' must be observed, and the *Community Rule* says the same thing. The 'covenanters' at Qumran regarded themselves as a faithful remnant upholding the law of Moses under the Master of Righteousness. 'All those who embrace the *Community Rule*,' it was decreed, 'shall enter into the covenant before God to obey all his commandments and not to abandon him during the dominion of Satan because of fear of terror or affliction.'[13]

The *Rule* then gives the ritual for entering the covenant. It is based on Deuteronomy 27–30 and consists of benedictions and the warnings which accompanied the giving of the Law on Sinai.

In his edition of the Dead Sea Scrolls, Geza Vermes suggests that the community gathered at Pentecost to receive new members and that some of the hymns which have been translated were used on this occasion. Hymn 21 expressly refers to the oath of the covenant:

'Thou hast shed thy Holy Spirit upon me
and thus drawn me nearer to understanding thee.
And the closer I approach,
the more am I filled with zeal
against all the workers of iniquity
and the men of deceit. . . .

For none of those who approach thee
rebels against thy command,
nor do any of those who know thee
alter thy words;
for thou art just,
and all thine elect are truth.
Thou wilt blot out all wickedness and sin for ever,
and thy righteousness shall be revealed
before the eyes of all thy creatures.

[12] G. R. Driver, *The Judaean Scrolls*, pp. 316ff.
[13] c. 1., G. Vermes, *The Dead Sea Scrolls in English*, p. 72.

B

I know through thy great goodness
and with an oath I have undertaken
never to sin against thee,
nor to do anything evil in thine eyes.
And thus do I bring into community
all the men of my Council.[14]

In his *De vita contemplativa* Philo, who lived from about
20 B.C. to about A.D. 45, mainly in Alexandria, gives an
account of another Jewish semi-monastic sect who held the
feast of Pentecost in veneration. These were the Therapeuts,
whose communities were to be found in Egypt on the shores
of Lake Mareotis not far from Alexandria and whom he
knew quite well:

'First of all the people assemble after seven sets of seven
days have passed, for they revere not only the simple seven
but its square also, since they know its chastity and perpetual
virginity. This is the eve of the chief feast which Fifty
(*pentecostas*) takes for its own—Fifty, the most sacred of
numbers and the most deeply rooted in nature.' [15]

The evidence of the *Book of Jubilees*, the Dead Sea Scrolls,
and Philo, therefore, indicates that the feast of Pentecost
became popular among the sects of Judaism as a commemoration of the giving of the Law on Sinai. It is not until the
second and third centuries A.D. that this association was made
by the rabbis of orthodox Judaism (in Rabbi Jose ben
Chalapta *c.* 150 and in Rabbi El'eazar ben Pedath *c.* 270).
But by then Pentecost had assumed a newer and more
dynamic significance in that greatest of all Jewish sects, the
Christian Church.[16]

[14] ibid., pp. 192–3.
[15] *De vita contemplativa*, 65 (Leob Classics, ix, pp. 151–2).
[16] I have not discussed the association of the feast of Tabernacles
with the period when Israel was in tents in the wilderness. It has no
particular relevance to our subject, and as a festival Tabernacles
has no successor in the Church's calendar. It was not, however,
without significance: see J. Danielou, *Primitive Christian Symbols*,
chapter 1.

18

II. *The Great Sunday*

The Church's first calendar was an uncomplicated affair—so uncomplicated that its sheer simplicity might be mistaken for poverty. It consisted of a weekly observance not unlike the Jewish sabbath and a christianized version of the feast of Passover; and that was all.

The weekly observance can be traced back to New Testament times. Paul looked on 'the first day of the week' as the proper occasion for the assembly of the local Christian community. In Jewish societies the sabbath was the only free day, so it is probable that Christians began keeping the first day of the week by prolonging the sabbath into the night of Saturday–Sunday. The incident at Troas, when Paul addressed a gathering until well past midnight and then broke bread, suggests something like this. The author of the book of Revelation refers to 'the Lord's Day' and by the second century it was a well-known feature of Christian life. 'On the day which is called the Sun's Day,' wrote Justin (*d. c.* 165), 'there is an assembly of all who live in the towns or in the country . . . because it is the first day, on which God put to flight darkness and chaos and made the world; and on the same day Jesus Christ our Saviour rose from the dead.' [1]

Lack of evidence about the origins of the Christian Passover—we will call it the Pasch unless it is more convenient to refer to it by its Saxon name, Easter—has created one of the minor problems of liturgical scholarship. If the Church celebrated the triumph of Christ each week, why did it adopt a Jewish festival as well—especially since, according to the New Testament writers, this festival was only a prefiguring of all that had been accomplished in Christ?

The old observance was, of course, closely intertwined with Christian teaching and devotion. Much of the Gospel is presented in paschal terms. Yet the only hint that Passover might have been celebrated in the New Testament Church

[1] *Apologia*, lxvii (*The Early Christian Fathers*, ed. H. Bettenson, p. 59).

as a Christian feast is in Paul's letter to Corinth. Urging his readers to root out a sinner from their assembly, he told them, 'Then you will be bread of a new baking, as it were unleavened Passover bread. For indeed our Passover has begun; the sacrifice is offered—Christ himself. So we who observe the festival must not use the old leaven, the leaven of corruption and wickedness, but only the unleavened bread of sincerity and truth.' [2] Many commentators feel, however, that Paul was referring only to the paschal nature of the eucharistic assembly, not to any annual festival.

An attempt to find a solution to the problem has been made by tracing back to its origins the controversy over the date of the Pasch in the early Church. It is a well-known fact of Church history that the congregations in Asia nearly created a schism at the end of the apostolic era because they thought, 'according to a very old tradition, that the feast of the Saviour's Pasch ought to be kept on the fourteenth day of the moon, and that therefore, on whatever day of the week this might fall, it was essential to end the time of fasting then.' [3] In view of this it has been suggested that in some Judaeo-Christian congregations the Passover was still kept in its old form and that these customs were carried over into the Church of the Gentiles after the final breach with the synagogue. In this manner the feast of Passover would have become the first Christian festival.

Be this as it may, what gave the Pasch its real importance for the Church by the end of the second century was that it became the normal occasion in the year for admitting the catechumens to baptism and the eucharist. Their long preparation culminated in the strict fast of two or three days in what we now call Holy Week. The night of Holy Saturday, the beginning of the Pasch, was kept as a vigil with readings and prayers. At cock-crow the candidates went to the place of baptism and undressed. They made their renunciation of Satan and were anointed with the oil of exorcism. Finally they were baptized and received their first Communion at sunrise on Easter Day. Admittedly, the process by which the rites of the New Testament Church developed into the liturgy described by Hippolytus in the *Apostolic Tradition* is obscure, and there is no reason to suppose that the development was

[2] 1 Corinthians 5:7–8.
[3] Eusebius, *Eccl. Hist.*, V, 23 (Penguin Classics edition, p. 230).

the same everywhere; but it is not difficult to see that, as the day when the new members participated sacramentally in Christ's baptismal death and resurrection, Easter would have a special prominence in the life of the Church.

The name 'Pentecost' appears in the New Testament and in early Christian writings, but it was not until the latter half of the second century that the name was used to refer to a Christian celebration as distinct from the Jewish one.

The earliest references of this kind come from widely scattered places, so we will take a rapid, imaginary tour round the Mediterranean, collecting them together and seeing how the word was used.

Our first source is a book on the Pasch by Irenaeus, who was Bishop of Lyons in southern Gaul and who was martyred about A.D. 200. Since Irenaeus is known to have followed the customs of the Roman Church, it is probable that this source reflects the usage not only of his own see but also that of the Church in the imperial capital as well. No actual copy of the book has survived, but it is mentioned in a fifth century work called *Quaestiones et responsiones ad orthodoxos* by an unknown Syrian author:

'On Sunday one does not kneel to pray as a sign of the resurrection which, by the grace of Christ, frees us both from sins and from death which has been destroyed with them. This custom originated in the apostles' time, according to the blessed martyr, Irenaeus, Bishop of Lyons, who in his book on the Pasch mentions that Pentecost was a time when one does not kneel. This has the same significance as Sunday, for the reason we have given.' [4]

'Pentecost' in this context does not seem to be the name of a Sunday. If it had been a title, there would have been no point in describing it as a time when one stood for prayer, since in the early Church one was expected to stand for prayer on Sundays anyway.

The apocryphal book, the *Acts of Paul*, was written about the same period. It was known to Tertullian as a work by a

[4] F. Cabrol and H. Leclercq, *Monumenta Ecclesiae Liturgica*, 1, 2259, and quoted in R. Cabié, *La Pentecôte: l'évolution de la Cinquantaine Pascale au cours des cinq premiers siècles*, p. 37. I must take this opportunity of acknowledging my debt to this latter book, recently published by Desclée (1965). Besides Fr. Cabié's own comments, I found particularly convenient the copious quotations from early sources which he has carefully assembled in the footnotes.

presbyter in Asia Minor. After describing how the apostle Paul had been condemned to the wild beasts, the author added, 'Now as it was Pentecost the brethren did not mourn or bow their knees, but rejoiced and prayed standing.'[5] The story is, of course, legendary: it was presumably based on Paul's remarks about fighting with wild beasts at Ephesus. But it is interesting from our point of view, because the unknown presbyter seems to have unconsciously projected into his narrative ideas about Pentecost from the customs with which he was familiar. Like Irenaeus, he hardly seems to use the name to describe a particular Sunday.

Origen (d. c. 245) is a difficult writer to interpret for he was more interested in the mystical and eschatological significance of Jewish and Christian observances than in liturgical details, but in his reply to the pagan philosopher, Celsus, which we shall quote from again later, he used the phrase, 'in the days of Pentecost.' Origen's life was spent in Egypt and Palestine, so we may assume that in those parts the name Pentecost also referred to a period rather than to a single day.

It is Tertullian (d. c. 220) who gives us the earliest exposition of what Pentecost meant as a Christian festival. Tertullian was a catechist in north Africa over the turn of the century and references to Pentecost appear in several of his works.

Some Christian communities apparently refrained from kneeling for prayer on Saturdays as well as Sundays and, discussing this, he wrote:

'But for us, according to our tradition, it is only on the day of the Lord's resurrection that we must not do this, nor allow any anxieties to overcome our spirit and activities; we put off even our daily business lest we give place to the devil. It is the same during the season of Pentecost (spatium pentecostes) which is noted as a similar time of rejoicing.'

On another occasion, criticizing those Christians who joined in pagan celebrations, he argued that if the situation was reversed, the heathen would never join in the Church's festivities; and then he added rhetorically:

'Not the Lord's Day, not Pentecost, even if they had known them, would they have shared with us; for they would fear lest they should appear to be Christian! . . . If you take all their public festivals and put them side by side, they could not make up a Pentecost!'

[5] E. Hennecke, New Testament Apocrypha, vol. ii, p. 370.

The name Pentecost is used in these quotations to refer to a season, not to a single day like the feast of Weeks. It is something novel, a season of fifty days:

'If there is a new creation in Christ, our celebrations must also be new: else if the apostle had completely erased all devotions "of seasons, and days, and months, and years," why do we celebrate the Pasch each year during the first month? And why in the following fifty days do we spend all our time rejoicing?'

In *De baptismo* there occurs Tertullian's famous description of Pentecost. He was explaining that, if Easter is the most suitable time for baptisms, so also are the days after it:

'Pentecost is the most joyful season (*laetissimum spatium*) for the administration of baptism. It is the time when the Lord's resurrection was made widely known among the disciples, when the gift of the Holy Spirit was inaugurated, and when the hope of the Lord's second coming was revealed. It is the time when, after his ascension into heaven, the angels told the apostles that he would return as he had gone up into heaven, that is, at Pentecost. And when Jeremiah said, "I will gather them together from the farthest parts of the earth on a feast day," he meant by that the Pasch and Pentecost, which is truly a festal day.'

As it is a most joyful season, fasting is suspended:

'We believe that neither fasting nor kneeling in adoration is allowed on Sunday: the same exemption applies as we rejoice from the Pasch throughout Pentecost (*in Pentecosten usque*).' [6]

This is why Hippolytus, recording the discipline of the Roman Church, said that any one who had accidentally missed keeping the fast before the Pasch should compensate for the omission by fasting, not during Pentecost, but afterwards:

'If any one is pregnant or sick and cannot fast the two days' (the Thursday and Friday of what we now call Holy Week) 'let them fast on the Saturday, taking bread and water if necessary. . . . But if any one be at sea or by reason of any necessity did not know the right day, when he has learned it, let him fast in compensation after Pentecost.' [7]

[6] The quotations are from *De Oratione* xxiii, 2; *De Idololatria* xiv, 7; *De Ieiunio* xiv, 2; *De Baptismo* xix, 2; *De Corona* iii, 4. The interpretation of Tertullian's view given here is the opposite of that made in J. A. MacArthur, *The Evolution of the Christian Year*, p. 151.

[7] *The Apostolic Tradition*, xxix, ed. G. Dix, p. 56.

What little evidence there is, then, indicates that in Gaul, Rome, Asia Minor, Palestine, Egypt and North Africa, Pentecost was the title given to the season of fifty days following Easter. During this season the Church rejoiced in the salvation wrought by Christ and her members did not kneel to pray, nor did they fast, because these acts of penitence were considered unsuitable at such a time. True to this tradition, the Council of Nicaea (325) laid down in its twentieth canon:

'Since there are some persons who kneel on the Lord's Day and in the days of Pentecost: in order that all things may be observed in like manner in every parish, the holy synod has decreed that all should at those times offer up their prayers to God standing.' [8]

It is after Nicaea that we find, in the *Festal Letters* of Athanasius, the most vivid exposition of the meaning of these great Fifty Days. The main purpose of the letters, written between the years 329 and 373, was to inform other bishops under the patriarchate of Alexandria the precise date on which Easter was to be kept each year, but Athanasius reveals his thoughts on the season by phrases which occur in them.

By keeping the great Fifty Days, he said, 'we shall be heirs of the kingdom of heaven,' for the feast was a 'symbol of the world to come' and a means by which God made known 'the joy and everlasting rest prepared in heaven for us.' It was 'the holy Pentecost, passing on to which, as through a succession of feasts, let us keep festival to the Spirit.' The result would be a more joyful Christian life for the remainder of the year: 'The Sun of Righteousness, causing his divine beams to rise upon us, proclaims beforehand the time of the feast in which, obeying him, we ought to celebrate it; so that when the time has passed away, gladness likewise may not leave us. . . . It behoves us, then, to rejoice and be glad with the joy that arises from good works, during the seven weeks which remain, giving glory to the Father and saying, "This is the day which the Lord hath made: we will rejoice and be glad in it." ' [9]

A common feature of the quotations we have collected is

[8] Quoted in J. Stevenson, *A New Eusebius*, p. 364. In the fourth century a 'parish' was a local church under the pastoral care of a bishop—roughly corresponding to the modern diocese, though usually much smaller.

[9] *The Festal Letters of St. Athanasius* (Library of the Fathers), pp. 80ff.

the way in which their authors compare the great Fifty Days to the first day of the week. It was the most joyful season that had 'the same significance as Sunday' (Irenaeus); it was 'a festal day' (Tertullian) or 'a succession of feasts' (Athanasius) that enjoyed the same liturgical and disciplinary privileges as the Lord's Day. It is probably a coincidence that the period is roughly one-seventh of the year, but in early Christian estimation the season of Pentecost was to the year what Sunday was to the week. In fact, Athanasius called it (in the Latin version of his letters) *magna dominica*, 'the great Sunday.'

By this time Sunday had come to be interpreted in the seven-day cycle as a sacramental realization of eternal life, the eternal 'to-day' of the people of God expounded by the author of Hebrews. That is why it was referred to as both the first day and the *eighth* day. Seven days were a figure of temporal life, the eighth day a figure of eternity. 'The first day is also the eighth day, denoting completeness,' said Justin. Basil, Bishop of Caesarea in Cappadocia (*c.* 330–79), recalled that the Lord's Day was both the day of resurrection and the day of the age to come: 'It is in virtue of an authoritative claim that the Church teaches her children to say their prayers standing on this day so that, by a perpetual recalling of eternal life, we may not neglect the means that lead us to it.' [10]

The old Pentecost taught the same lesson in the cycle of the years. The Pasch was not just a commemoration of the resurrection, as Easter is to us: it was a *passage* to the new life opened for Christians through the passion, resurrection and ascension of Jesus Christ and the coming of the Holy Spirit; it was a liturgical introduction to a season of fifty festal days during which the Church, together with those who had been baptized during the paschal vigil, rejoiced in her salvation and looked for the second coming of the Lord. 'What we to-day call Eastertide and which appears in our calendar as the *pascha Domini*,' wrote Dom Odo Casel, the famous liturgical scholar of Maria Laach, 'the first Christians had already named Pentecost.' [11]

Ephesians 2: 6–7 was not, as far as we know, written with the significance of Sunday and of the great Fifty Days in mind, yet these verses reflect exactly the meaning of the

[10] *De Spir. Sanct.*, 27.
[11] Quoted by Cabié, p. 52.

25

observances: 'In union with Christ Jesus God raised us up and enthroned us with him in the heavenly realms, so that he might display in the ages to come how immense are the resources of his grace, and how great his kindness to us in Christ Jesus.'

Pentecost was a symbol of the paschal mystery in its fulfilment. It portrayed the fruition of the Christian hope—a harvest such as the feast of Weeks had prefigured only as a shadow. During these days the Church celebrated the paschal offering of Christ, 'the firstfruits of the harvest of the dead,' and her members rejoiced in their exaltation with him. Among them in the eucharistic assembly were the newly-baptized, the fruits of the Church's mission, ready-gathered by the sacrament of initiation for the greatest harvest at the end of the world. These were days of a 'joy in harvest' of a profoundly spiritual kind.

The Fathers saw in the number of the days a promise of forgiveness and redemption. In Jewish thought eight (7 plus 1) is more perfectly realized in fifty (7 times 7 plus 1) and the Old Testament knew this amplification of the sabbath in its prescription for a 'year of jubilee' every fiftieth year. It was supposed to be a year when liberty was proclaimed to the captives, slaves were released, and every man returned to his own family and his own property. It is not likely the year of jubilee was observed very faithfully, but the implications of it fascinated Christian writers. Origen called fifty 'the number sacred to forgiveness and remission,' and Basil, after the passage about Sunday as a 'recalling of eternal life,' continued:

'Moreover, all Pentecost is a reminder of the resurrection expected in the age to come. For that one and first day, if seven times multiplied by seven, completes the seven weeks of the holy Pentecost; for, beginning at the first, Pentecost ends with the same (i.e. Sunday), making fifty revolutions through the like intervening days. And so it is a likeness of eternity, beginning and ending as it does in a circling course at the same point. On this day the rules of the Church have led us to prefer the upright attitude of prayer, for by their clear prompting they make our mind no longer dwell in the present but in the future.' [12]

As a 'reminder of the resurrection,' the great Fifty Days

[12] *De Spir. Sanct.*, 27.

were also an earnest of the marriage feast of heaven, and some of the Fathers pointed out that this was the reason why fasting was suspended. They applied to the most joyful season the answer to our Lord's question, ' "Can you make the bridegroom's friends fast while the bridegroom is with them?" ' Eusebius, Bishop of Caesarea (c. 260–c. 340) explained, 'In the holy days of Pentecost, prefiguring the future rest, we rejoice our souls and relax our bodies as if we are united with him who is now the Bridegroom, and we cannot fast.' [13]

But we must not read too much into the references of the early Pentecost. Except for those who lived in the close intimacy of a community, the early Christians were in no position to have seven weeks' holiday each year. Daily life must have continued its normal course during the period as at other times. Perhaps the more wealthy and leisured among the Christian groups were able to savour the variation in their routine of prayer and discipline—liturgical and other religious observances have a way of flourishing among those who have nothing much else to do!—but mainly it was a spiritual joy, outwardly expressed in standing for prayer and in a suspension of all fasting. Its effect was to help the Christian realize what salvation meant in the terms of his ordinary life as, redeemed and forgiven in Christ, he was united to the Godhead in the fellowship of the Holy Spirit.

How the title of a Jewish festival came to be attached to a Christian festive season we can only guess. Words borrowed from Hellenistic Judaism were given a newer and, for us, more significant meaning by the early Church. *Ecclesia, pascha, gratia* and other terms came into the Christian vocabulary, illuminated by the New Testament and sanctified by the faith of the Church. *Pentecost* was yet another, reinterpreted in the new dispensation of Christ. Yet perhaps the Christian feast day was not so far removed from the Jewish one. Although Pentecost was the title given to the feast of Weeks in circles outside priestly Judaism, the festival itself, as the completion of the grain harvest, looked back over the intervening days to Passover-Unleavened Bread when the harvest had begun. The Christian church appropriated and fulfilled the ancient observance in its own characteristc way.

---

[13] *De solemnitate paschali*, 3, quoted in the *Dictionnaire d'Archéologie Chrétienne et de Liturgie*, ed. F. Cabrol &c., vol. 14, p. 267.

Interestingly, this conception of Pentecost has left its mark on the way some of the Fathers quoted the passage in Acts 2 describing the descent of the Holy Spirit on the disciples in Jerusalem. The Greek version of the first verse of this chapter reads, 'When the *day* of Pentecost was being completed' (*Kai en tō sumplērousthai tēn hēmeran tēs pentēkostēs*). In some Latin versions, however, this has become, 'When the *days* of Pentecost were being completed.' Augustine always used the singular when he quoted this verse except in the *Epistula ad catholicos* (but the Augustinian authorship of this work is disputed). 'Day' is found in the *Liber de promissionibus*, attributed to Quodvultdeus, a disciple of the Bishop of Hippo. But Gregory of Elvira (*d. c.* 392) quoted the verse twice with the word in the plural in *Tractatus Origenis*. A little later Jerome employed 'days' in two of his letters and in his translation of the Bible, completed about 404. And so it remains, *Cum complerentur dies pentecostes*, in the Vulgate down to the present time—a relic of a form of Pentecost long since forgotten.

III. *Social and Doctrinal Influences*

Though the early Christian calendar was an unsophisticated affair, then, it was anything but impoverished. Its simplicity enfolded the greatest riches of the Church's faith. In the weekly cycle of the Sundays and in the yearly cycle of the Paschs and the Pentecosts, her members rejoiced in their deliverance from the bondage of sin, of time, and of mortality, into 'the liberty and splendour of the children of God' and 'the eternal kingdom of our Lord and Saviour Jesus Christ.' [1]

This is not, of course, the historical and commemorative calendar that we know to-day. But the early Christians had little interest in observances that rooted them in the present age. Their outlook was eschatological. The events in salvation-history were only relevant to them because salvation was a here-and-now event. They regarded themselves as sojourners on a pilgrimage through the present world which would end with the consummation of all things in Christ, and it was in the joy of this conviction that they stood for prayers and suspended all fasting on Sundays and during the great Fifty Days, because these were an earnest, a foretaste, of the triumphant life in God's kingdom.

Besides, the first generations of Christians associated festivals with the pagan observances of the Roman empire. It is calculated that at the beginning of the third century there were in Rome about one hundred and seventy-five public holidays each year, many of them having a religious significance, and all of them devoted to games in the circus, plays in the theatre, and excesses of various kinds. The Church had no inclination to copy these. Indeed, her members were particularly sensitive to the criticism that their observances were the same as pagan feasts. In his reply to Celsus, Origen insisted:

'If any one makes a rejoinder to this by talking about our observances on certain days, the Lord's Day which we keep, or the Preparation, or the Pasch, or the Pentecost, we would

[1] Romans 8:21; 2 Peter 1:11.

reply to this that the perfect man, who is always engaged in the words, works and thoughts of the divine Logos, who is by nature his Lord, is always living in his days and is continually observing the Lord's Day. Moreover, since he is always making himself ready for the true life and abstaining from the pleasures of this life which deceive the multitude, and since he does not nourish "the mind of the flesh," but buffets his body and makes it his slave, he is always observing the Preparation. Furthermore, if a man has understood that "Christ our Passover was sacrificed," and that he ought to "keep the feast" by eating the flesh of the Logos, there is not a moment when he is not keeping the Pasch, which means offerings before making a crossing. For he is always passing over in thought and in every word and every deed from the affairs of this life to God and hastening towards his city. In addition to this, if a man is able to say truthfully "we are risen with Christ," and also that "he raised us up and made us sit with him in heavenly places in Christ," he is always living in the days of Pentecost, and particularly when, like the apostles of Jesus, he goes up to the upper room and gives time to supplication and prayer, so that he is worthy of the mighty rushing wind from heaven which compels the evil in men and its consequences to disappear, and so that he becomes worthy also of some share in the fiery tongue given by God.' [2]

But a century after Origen's death things began to change. The fourth century was in many ways a turning-point in the life of the Church. It brought to an end the threat of persecution and saw the beginning of the Church-State alliance that was to have such a profound effect on both institutions. If the State was partially christianized, it is equally true that the Church was partially moulded by the patterns of secular thought and society. Its members were less and less inclined to think of themselves as having no permanent home in this life and as seekers after the city which is to come. The peace of Constantine had given them a place in this world's existence, and the Church was taking the form of an earthly kingdom. Membership was thrown open to all, and the lead given by Christian rulers and governors brought tens of thousands flocking into the Church. By the year 410 Christians could sing, in the words of what was then a new hymn,

[2] *Contra Celsum*, viii, 22, ed. H. Chadwick (1953), p. 468.

30

'All the earth doth worship thee: the Father everlasting' (the *Te Deum*).

One important result was that social life was adjusted to the rhythm of the Christian week and the Christian year. Constantine allowed his soldiers to be excused duty on Sundays so that they could join in the Church's worship, and under his successors games in the circus, plays in the theatre, and trials in the courts were forbidden on this day. The Christian way of life—at least, in its outward appearances—was being supported by the powers that be.

It was from about this time that the obligation of attending mass on the Lord's Day began to appear in the ecclesiastical canons, and fine new basilicas were built in cities and towns to accommodate the crowds of worshippers. These in turn encouraged the clergy to celebrate the liturgy with more splendid ceremonial, and as part of this process the calendar developed. Some items were appropriated from the pagan calendar. It was sound missionary tactics to baptize December 25th as the festival of Christ's birth. The popular observance of the winter solstice was brought within the orbit of the Church's faith and practice.

But the calendar was not elaborated just to bring the Church's mission to society. Dogma was also involved. The Church had for long found herself under pressure to defend the Gospel—and especially her beliefs about the nature and the person of Jesus Christ—from the inroads of heresy, and just as the human birth of Christ proclaimed the reality of his manhood, so his bodily ascent to heaven proclaimed the eternal union of God and man in heaven. These events are the alpha and the omega of the incarnate Lord's work on earth. The ascension also proclaimed Christ's total victory over the principalities and powers above and below. The concept of a three-decker cosmos (as a philosophical concept if not a cosmological one) made it necessary to teach that our Lord had triumphed over evil in the upper and the lower realms. His descent into hell and his ascent into heaven was the Church's answer to this question on the agenda of contemporary philosophy.

Similarly, disputes about the Holy Spirit prompted the formation of the Church's doctrine on the Third Person of the Holy Trinity. The Nicene Creed merely affirmed belief 'in the Holy Spirit,' but during the latter half of the century the Spirit's position within the Godhead was more closely defined. It was a matter which occupied the attention of the Cappadocian Fathers in the East—Basil the Great, Gregory, Bishop of Nazianzus (*d.* 389) and Gregory, Bishop of Nyssa (*d. c.* 395)—and in the West, Augustine, Bishop of Hippo (*d.* 430). The debate reached its climax at the Council of Constantinople (381) when the consubstantiality of the Holy Spirit as well as that of the Son was formally endorsed by the Church. Some years later Augustine published *De Trinitate*, in which he accepted without question that there is one God who is Trinity and that Father, Son and Holy Spirit are at once distinct and co-essential but numerically one.[3]

Definitions like these highlighted the sequence in the economy of salvation. Since it was only after the man Jesus had been perfected in obedience to the Father that his sacrifice could be accepted and the Holy Spirit sent, the totality of the saving act of God in Christ began to be more marked by its stages. In St. John's Gospel, for example, the ordered procession in the work of Father, Son and Holy Spirit is very clearly distinguished ('The Spirit had not yet been given, because Jesus had not yet been glorified . . .') and the same procession is implied in Acts. (' "The Jesus we speak of has been raised by God, as we can all bear witness. Exalted thus at God's right hand, he received the Holy Spirit from the Father, as was promised, and all you now see and hear flows from him." ')[4] What the great Fifty Days symbolized in their entirety was now split up and its constituents attached to separate days within the season.

We might ask, why did the Church not recognize from the beginning the forty and fifty days' intervals between the resurrection, the ascension, and the coming of the Holy Spirit? But to ask that question is to reveal the limitations of our modern outlook. We are so used to keeping Ascension Day and Whitsunday that we have forgotten the events which these festivals celebrate are by no means as detached and

[3] J. N. D. Kelly, *Early Christian Doctrine*, pp. 255ff. It was Augustine who taught, more unequivocally than any of the Western Fathers before him, the doctrine of the double procession of the Spirit from the Father and the Son (*filioque*) in distinction from Gregory of Nyssa's teaching that the Holy Spirit processed 'out of the Father through the Son'—thus cutting the rift that was to widen between Eastern and Western Christendom in later centuries.

[4] John 7:39; Acts 2:32–3.

distinct in the New Testament as we assume. If we read Mark 16: 19 and Luke 24: 50-1 with fresh eyes, we get the impression that the ascension took place on the eve of the first day of the week as part of the resurrection event, while John 20: 17-22 implies that not only the ascension but also the gift of the Spirit occurred on Easter Day. It is only when we study Acts 1 and 2 that the familiar intervals emerge.

There is yet another problem. What kind of evidence must we look for before we decide that a day was kept by the early Church as a festival in the normal sense of the word? The most reliable witnesses, of course, are the first lectionaries with their titles for certain days and their provision of suitable pericopes; but before they appear we have to rely on more sketchy clues. References may be misleading. For example, the canons of the Council of Elvira, which met in Spain in 313, refer to 'the day of Pentecost,' but there is no indication that the bishops were thinking of that day as a festival in the liturgical sense. Again, the fact that a sermon was given on a Christian mystery does not mean that the day on which it was delivered was a feast in honour of it. In the last quarter of the century a homily now attributed to Gregory, Bishop of Elvira, mentions the fact that Acts 2 has just been read as a lection in the service and seems to suggest that on that day (it is not clear *which* day, the feast of Weeks in Acts 2 or the day of the sermon [5]) the Holy Spirit descended upon the Church. Is this evidence of an early celebration of Whitsunday, or is it just a rhetorical passage from an expository sermon?

With these considerations in mind, we can now turn to the first movement in the evolution of the great Fifty Days—an emphasis on the fiftieth and last day of Pentecost as the closing assembly of the feast.

Since it always fell on a Sunday, it is easy to see why this particular day should acquire an importance of its own. It was the day when the faithful were expected to be in church at the eucharist and when imperial law freed them from work to fulfil this obligation. What effect this had on the fiftieth day, however, is a matter of dispute among scholars. The evidence is slight and its interpretation is not always clear. Some scholars have suggested that the fiftieth day was a kind

[5] The doubt arises from the exact meaning of the sentence, *Hic est, inquam, Spiritus qui hac die, id est Pentecosten, a Deo ecclesiae missus est.*

of unitive feast day celebrating both the ascension and the gift of the Spirit: others have argued that this is to read too much into the evidence and that in any case an ascension festival is to be found elsewhere on the fortieth day at about the same time.

Four chapters of Fr. Cabié's book deal with this problem. We can only indicate very briefly the scope of the discussion here.

First, he collects material to show that in some parts of the fourth-century Church the fiftieth day was used to commemorate the gift of the Spirit. He quotes sources from Constantinople, Rome, and Milan (as well as from Spain, which we have just mentioned).

Gregory of Nazianzus preached about 379 on the symbolism of the number seven and of fifty as denoting 'the one day which we have partaken from the age to come and which is itself the eighth and the first or, rather, the one and indestructible day'—the older significance of the great Fifty Days—and then went on, 'We celebrate Pentecost, when the Spirit rests upon us, the appointed day for the promise, the fulfilment of hope. . . . A breathing which is the breath of God and a present share in the tongues of fire.' [6]

In Rome a writer known as Ambrosiaster, who lived during the pontificate of Damasus (366–84), answered in *Questiones veteris et novi testamenti* a query about Pentecost:

'Pentecost, which is fixed on the fiftieth day after Easter, has this significance: just as after seven days the first day is Sunday, in which is fulfilled the paschal mystery for the redemption and salvation of mankind . . . so also after seven weeks the first day is Pentecost. And Pentecost can fall on no other day than a Sunday, because it is known that everything which concerns the salvation of mankind both began and was fulfilled on the Lord's Day.'

Ambrosiaster went on to draw out the typology of the Old Testament in a way which associated the fiftieth day with the gift of the Holy Spirit:

'Just as the lamb was a figure of the Lord's passion in the sacrament of Easter, so the giving of the Law was a prefiguring of the Gospel. Because on that same day, that is, Pentecost, the Law was given, the Holy Spirit descended on

[6] *Oratio XLI*, Cabié, p. 118.

the disciples giving them authority and wisdom to preach the Gospel.'[7]

In *De apologia prophetae David*, written about 384, Ambrose expounded the symbolism of fifty, showing how it signified a remission of debts and a restoration of possessions according to the regulations of the year of jubilee, and then he went on to affirm that the Christian is similarly freed from sin through Christ's passion and rejoices in his freedom during the days after Easter: 'And we receive the grace of the Holy Spirit who comes to us on the day of Pentecost. Fasting ceases, God is praised, and "Alleluia" is sung.'[8]

Next, Fr. Cabié marshals quotations that seem to associate the fiftieth day with the ascension of Christ.

Eusebius called the fiftieth day the 'seal' of Pentecost and linked it with the ascension:

'The pentecostal number does not stop at these seven weeks but, beyond them, at the final number which follows, comes the seal of the solemn day of the Lord's ascension.'

(However, when he used the expression again in his *Vita Constantini* he mentioned both the ascension and the gift of the Holy Spirit:

'All these events' (he had described Constantine's baptism) 'occurred during a most important festival, I mean the august and holy solemnity of Pentecost (distinguished by a period of seven weeks, and sealed by one day) during which the holy scriptures attest the ascension of our common Saviour into heaven and the descent of the Holy Spirit among men. In the course of this feast the emperor received the privileges I have just described; and on the last day of all, which one might justly call the feast of feasts, he was removed about midday to the presence of God.'[9])

The *Doctrina Apostolorum*, a series of twenty-seven canons, with pseudo-historical notes, purports to contain the instructions given by our Lord when he sent the eleven apostles on their mission to the world. It is probable that this work came from the Church in Syria and it is dated about the beginning

[7] ibid., pp. 120–1.
[8] ibid., p. 122.
[9] *Vita Constantini*, IV, 64 (*Nicene and Post-Nicene Fathers*, p. 557). The Bishop of Caesarea was no literary stylist, so we must not interpret 'the feast of feasts' too strictly in terms of liturgical observance. Also, we must remember he was writing a panegyric for his patron.

of the fourth century. After the descent of the Holy Spirit, the apostles are supposed to have promulgated certain disciplinary and liturgical canons for the benefit of the whole Church, and one of these (No. 9) ran:

'Furthermore, the apostles laid down that when the fifty days after the resurrection were fulfilled, the commemoration would be made of his ascension to his glorious Father.' [10]

(Another version of the manuscript has 'forty' instead of 'fifty,' but Fr. Cabié argues that this is a later alteration. To substantiate this he refers to a Syriac lectionary of the late fifth century published by F. C. Burkitt in the *Proceedings of the British Academy,* vol. II (1923), from a manuscript in the British Museum, giving two sets of lections, one for the 'Ascension of our Lord unto his glorious Father' and the other for the 'Sunday of the completion of Pentecost.' Fr. Cabié suggests that the two sets of lections were originally part of one list which was a lectionary for the fiftieth day with readings for the ascension and for the gift of the Holy Spirit. The argument is based on a comparison of the various pericopes; and if it is correct, it is further evidence that both events were once associated with the last day of Pentecost.)

Lactanius, a Christian apologist (*c.* 240–*c.* 320), twice mentioned the ascension on the fortieth day, but some versions have *quinquagesima die*. Epiphanius, Bishop of Salamis (*c.* 315–*c.* 403), spoke of Christ the first-fruits returning to heaven on the last day of Pentecost. Maximus, Bishop of Turin (*c.* 390–*c.* 470), has three homilies which were probably delivered on the fiftieth day which give prominence to the *sessio* of Christ:

'Christ the Lord, conqueror after his triumph over the devil, sitting at the Father's right hand, has to-day poured his gifts on his disciples—not of gold coins or of silver, but the heavenly blessings of the Holy Spirit.' [11]

It is impossible, concludes Fr. Cabié, to make any generalizations from this material. The different stresses on the ascension and kingship of Christ and on the gift of the Holy Spirit may be no more than a reflection of the different spiritualities among the writers or the local Churches of which they were members. He suggests that the fiftieth day acquired

---

[10] W. Cureton, *Ancient Syriac Documents,* p. 27.

[11] *Hom.* LVI, 3. (*Sessio* = the sitting of Christ at the right hand of the Father.)

an importance of its own, as we have said, because it was the last day of the most joyful season of Pentecost and a day when people attended church. It provided the preachers with an opportunity of reminding their hearers of all that the great Fifty Days symbolized, especially the reign of the ascended Christ and the indwelling presence of the Holy Spirit.

We have to wait until the beginning of the fifth century before we can be sure that Ascension Day and Whitsunday had taken their place as major festivals in the liturgical year.

IV. *Ascension Day*

The ascension and the *sessio* of Christ were, as we have seen, important doctrinal as well as devotional elements in the Church's teaching on the nature and person of our Lord. And doctrinally as well as devotionally the Church looked back to the Old Testament to understand the significance of these events—to the ascensions of Enoch and Elijah, to the vision of the Ancient of Days in Daniel 7, and to the Psalms.

Psalms 47, 97 and 99 provided chants for the Church's rejoicing in her ascended and ruling Head ('God is gone up with a merry noise: and the Lord with the sound of the trump'; 'Thou, O Lord, art higher than all that are in the earth: thou art exalted far above all gods'; 'The Lord is king . . . he sitteth between the cherubim'), but 24, 68 and 110 aided the Church's teaching of these events and so are an integral part, not only of the liturgy of the ascension, but also of its proclamation.

Psalm 24, used as a proof-text to demonstrate that it was as a man that Christ had ascended into heaven, scripted the dramatic dialogue which took place at the gates of heaven when the risen Lord approached in his human body that still carried the marks of the passion. The idea that what he had done had been kept a secret from the angels at the gate—at first they did not recognize him—springs from the statement in the New Testament that what God accomplished in Christ was hidden from the principalities and powers of the spiritual realm and only made known to them through the Church.

'When Christ rose from the dead and ascended into heaven,' wrote Justin, 'the princes established by God in the heavens were commanded to open the gates of the heavens, so that he who is the King of glory might enter in and ascend to sit at the right hand of the Father, until he has made his enemies his footstool. But when the princes of heaven saw him without beauty, honour or glory, they did not recognize him, and they said, "Who is the King of glory?" '

Irenaeus heard the angels asking the question in Isaiah 63:

'When he, the conqueror, came forward with his body risen from the dead, certain of the powers said, "Who is this that cometh from Edom, with crimsoned garments from Bozrah?"' 'The angels ascending with Christ answered them, "The Lord of hosts, he is the King of glory,"' said Athanasius, 'teaching this great mystery to those who were in the heavens—that he who had conquered the spiritual enemies is the King of glory.'[1]

Psalm 68 revealed that as a result of the ascension those trapped in the power of evil were released. The key verse is number eighteen: 'Thou art gone up on high, thou hast led captivity captive, and received gifts for men.' Origen commented: 'He began by chaining the demon, and having entered his house—hell—and having ascended from there into the heights, he led away captives those who rose again and entered with him into the heavenly Jerusalem.'[2]

Psalm 110, one of the enthronement psalms, taught the Church to see in the ascension of Christ the beginning of his triumphal reign at the right hand of the Father. According to Mark 12: 35, Jesus himself quoted it in the course of his teaching in the temple, and it is the basis of a number of passages in the New Testament that proclaim the resurrection, the ascension and the *sessio* of Christ.[3] The early Christian who expressed his faith by using such phrases as, 'Salvation through the resurrection of Jesus Christ, who entered heaven after receiving the submission of angelic authorities and powers, and is now at the right hand of God,'[4] understood

[1] *Apol.* xxxvi; *Dem.* 84; *Exp. Ps. 23*. (Quoted by J. Danielou, *The Bible and the Liturgy*, pp. 305–6.)

[2] *Comm. Rom. V* (Danielou, p. 312). When quoted by the author of Ephesians, this verse was altered so that it implied gifts were given not *from men* but *to men*: 'But unto every one of us was the grace given according to the measure of the gift of Christ. Wherefore he saith, "When he ascended on high, he led captivity captive, and gave gifts unto men (*tois anthrōpois*)."' The gifts listed are charisms 'for the perfecting of the saints, unto the work of ministering, unto the building up of the body of Christ.' This is not a deliberate modification of an Old Testament text. The author saw that the work of the Church is energized by the Spirit of God given through Christ to all its members: Christ had in this sense 'received gifts for men' within the Church, and because of his ascension the gifts of the Holy Spirit could be sent to empower the people who were members of his body.

[3] e.g., Romans 8: 34; Colossians 3: 1; Ephesians 1: 20; Acts 2: 30; 5: 30; 7: 55, etc.

[4] 1 Peter 3: 21–2.

39

them as implying that our Lord had beaten down all hostile powers opposed to him and to his Church. 'Sit thou on my right hand' became a common phrase in Christian catechesis to describe the purpose of the ascension and to stress the unity of the risen Christ within the life of the Holy Trinity.

The promise to 'make thine enemies thy footstool' was used to interpret the Ephesian passage about God the Father putting 'all things in subjection under his feet.' It had the effect of separating the ascension and the *parousia* and seeing more clearly the latter as a consequence of the former. Eusebius of Caesarea expounded the verse in this way:

'The "throne" means the royal dignity of Christ; the "sitting" means the immovable stability of his royal state; "at the right hand" means his participation in the blessings at the right hand of the Father. The Son indeed receives from the Father all the good and saving blessings of his right hand to distribute them.' [5]

The second verse ('The Lord shall send the rod of thy power out of Sion') was taken as a prophetic reference to the missionary work of the Church in the power of the Holy Spirit. The divine commission lies behind the use of this psalm in the sermon of Acts 2 and the passage from Ephesians 1 which we have just referred to, and it is implied in the ending of St. Mark: 'So then the Lord Jesus, after he had spoken to them, was received up into heaven, and sat down at the right hand of God. And they went forth and preached everywhere, the Lord working with them, and confirming the word by the signs that followed.'

'I think "the rod of thy power" in this passage means the preaching of the Gospel,' said Eusebius. 'This word, indeed, which announces the power of our Saviour and the economy of his work, is a sceptre symbolizing at the same time teaching and salvation.'

As the Church's teaching on the ascension unfolded in this way—and we have only touched on a rich seam of patristic exposition [6]—it began to find tangible expression in her worship. By the middle of the fourth century the great theme in Christian art was the ascended and ruling Christ, as the anti-Arian formula, 'God of God, King of Kings, Lord of

[5] *Comm. Ps. 23* (Danielou, p. 310).
[6] See J. G. Davies, *He Ascended into Heaven* (Bampton Lectures, 1958).

Lords,' took visible shape in sculpture, painting and mosaic. On the sarcophagus of Junius Bassus, prefect of the city of Rome, the ascended Christ is shown seated in the heavens between Peter and Paul, the blessed Son of God eternally youthful and radiant, his feet resting on the billowing cloak of the ancinet sky-god. The sarcophagus is dated from 359 and is now in the crypt of St. Peter's. In the apses of the new basilicas Christ was portrayed enthroned in glory, facing the worshipper in the mandala of light, the *Pantocrator*, ruling in the triumph of serene humility with his subjects, the redeemed, gathered around him. One of the earliest known examples is in St. Pudenziana in Rome (*c.* 400) where Christ sits holding a book, *Conservator ecclesiae S. Pudentianae,* receiving golden garlands of victory with the glorious cross and the heavenly Jerusalem in the background.

Similarly the ascension found its place in the Church's calendar. It was there, like its representations in art, to teach the faithful the truth about their Lord and to provide them with the opportunity of worshipping him in the saving event.

Fortunately, a number of sources have survived which enable us to follow the emergence of an Ascension Day celebration in the Church at Jerusalem from the end of the fourth century onwards, and these may be put together to illustrate how the festival evolved in one important and liturgically-conscious Christian community.

The first source is the *Peregrinatio Egeriae*. Egeria was an abbess or nun from Gallicia in north-west Spain who made a pilgrimage to the Holy Land. She visited the sacred sites, including Jerusalem, and from Constantinople wrote an account of what she had seen for the benefit of her sisters in religion at home.

Egeria's visit probably occurred during the pontificate of John, who succeeded Cyril as bishop in the year 386. By then Jerusalem had become a centre of Christian pilgrimage and devotion. Fifty years earlier Constantine had embarked on an ambitious building programme to raise churches over the sacred sites of the Gospel, and although his scheme was delayed by disputes among churchmen, by the time of Egeria's visit the Christian community was well organized to cater for pilgrims. Places hallowed by their real or supposed connection with the ministry, passion and triumph of Jesus Christ were fitted into a series of liturgical exercises that

41

sanctified local topography in a devotional treat for the visitors.

The main buildings were in the Marturium-Anastasis complex in the heart of the city, enshrining the sites of the crucifixion and the sepulchre. (To-day these sites are contained within the Church of the Holy Sepulchre.) Also in the city was Sion, or the Church of the Apostles, erected over the supposed location of the upper room. On the mount of Olives outside the walls was Eleona, a church built by Constantine's mother, Helena, over a cave where Jesus is thought to have taught his disciples, and at the summit the Imbomon, or the Church of the Ascension, designed in the form of an octagon and completed about 375.[7]

Egeria records that on the fiftieth day of Pentecost, the services began as usual on a Sunday. There was a vigil in the Anastasis from cockcrow until dawn and then the eucharist was celebrated in the Martyrium. with addresses from the bishop and some of the presbyters. On this particular day, however, the ceremonies were shortened so that every one could get to Sion before nine o'clock—the time was important, for it was at the third hour that the Holy Spirit descended on the disciples in the upper room:

'When they get there, that passage of the Acts of the Apostles is read describing how the Spirit came down that men of all languages might understand the things that were spoken; *postmodum fit ordine suo missa.*[8] Then the presbyters preach on the passage that has been read, for this is the same spot in Sion where the crowd gathered with the apostles after the Lord's passion when what we have read from Acts actually took place. *Postmodum fit ordine suo missa;* the offering is made there; the archdeacon raises his voice and says, as the congregation is dismissed, "Let us all be ready at twelve o'clock to-day in Eleona, in Imbomon." '

After breakfast, the crowds went up the Mount of Olives:

[7] See the sketches and diagrams printed in W. Telfer's introduction to *Cyril of Jerusalem and Nemesius of Emesa* (vol. 4 of the *Library of Christian Classics*), pp. 49 and 53, and in J. G. Davies, *Holy Week,* p. 26.

[8] 'Afterwards the dismissal takes place in due course.' At this period *missa* could mean a solemn dismissal of the congregation, or it could mean 'mass.' Opinions vary among scholars as to whether or not there was likely to be more than one mass in Jerusalem each day at the time of Egeria's visit. (Text in L. Duchesne, *Christian Worship: its Origins and Evolution,* pp. 515ff.)

'First they enter the Imbomon, the place where the Lord ascended into heaven, and the bishop and the presbyters sit there with all the people. Lessons are read, interspersed with hymns, chants and prayers, appropriate to the day and the place. From the Acts of the Apostles is read the passage describing the Lord's ascension into heaven after his resurrection. When this is finished, the catechumens and the faithful are blessed, and every one comes down about three o'clock.'

Egeria goes on to describe how the people went in procession, singing hymns, to Eleona, and from there back down the hill into the city. It was dark when, carrying torches, they arrived at the Martyrium for more prayers and blessings. Then they went on to the Anastasis and, finally, to Sion. The day's liturgy ended about midnight. No wonder she noticed that every one was very tired!

We must interpret the meaning of this liturgy in Jerusalem with caution. On a number of occasions services were held in each of the churches, the worshippers and pilgrims progressing from one to the other throughout the day. A service at the Imbomon was usual on Palm Sunday, Maundy Thursday, Easter Day and Easter Monday, so it would be incorrect to assume Egeria attended a special function commemorating the ascension on the fiftieth day. But in observances of this kind we have, as it were, Ascension Day and Whitsunday in embryo, especially in the readings and the sermons.

Our second source from this area is the *Rituale Armenorum*, which is dated from the middle of the fifth century. This confirms the account written by the Spanish nun. Stations were made *in die Sanctae Pentecostes* in the Martyrium, in Sion, and on the Mount of Olives. There is, however, one difference from the details in Egeria's diary. The reading from Acts in the Imbomon has been dropped and in its place is read John 14: 15–24 ('I will pray the Father and he shall give you another Comforter . . .'). It seems as if during the intervening years the fiftieth day was now wholly concerned with the gift of the Spirit, even though the traditional station on the Mount of Olives was still observed.

The third source, the manuscript of an *ordo* of the same kind as the *Rituale Armenorum*, found in the convent of St. James of Jerusalem, is dated from the late fifth or early sixth century. It provides readings for the fortieth day after Easter, Acts 1: 1–14 and Luke 24: 41–53, and chants from

Psalms 24 ('Lift up your heads, O ye gates') and Psalm 47 ('God is gone up with a merry noise'). It also directs that the 'Alleluia' is to be sung. Here, clearly, is an Ascension Day festival.

Finally, the *Georgian Kanonarion*, which gives us the Jerusalem liturgy at the beginning of the seventh century just before the submergence of that Church under Arab rule, shows that the ascension is definitely commemorated on the fortieth day with a procession up the Mount of Olives and readings from Amos 9: 5–6 ('He buildeth his chambers in the heavens') and from Acts 1: 1–14. Unfortunately a gap in the manuscript prevents us from knowing what the gospel lection was, but we may guess it was Luke 24: 41–53.[9]

Ascension Day may have been kept in other parts of Christendom much earlier than in Jerusalem. At the beginning of the fourth century the Council of Elvira laid down that Pentecost must be celebrated on the fiftieth, not the fortieth, day, indicating that some sort of observance was being held on the day of the future festival. There is the mysterious title *Tessarakoste* mentioned by the Council of Nicaea and probably referring to a day during the fourth week of Pentecost.[10] Furthermore, Egeria herself describes a vigil and a mass she attended at Bethlehem on the fortieth day after Easter. It is headed 'the Ascension Festival' in the extracts printed from her diary as an appendix to L. Duchesne's *Christian Worship*, but she does not specifically say that this is what it was she saw. One theory is that during the year she was there some local observance was held in Bethlehem which fell on the fortieth day, perhaps an event connected with the Nativity, such as the massacre of the Innocents (which was kept on a different day before it was fixed in the Christmas octave) or the dedication of the church there (it is known that the dedication festival, May 31st, fell on the fortieth day after Easter in the year 417). But J. G. Davies has argued persuasively that what Egeria took part in was an early celebration of Ascension Day. The least we can say, therefore, is that the question is unresolved.[11]

[9] *Journal of Theological Studies*, vol. 24 (1923), pp. 415ff.

[10] S. Salaville, 'La *Tessarakoste* du Ve Canon de Nicée' in *Echoes d'Oriente*, pp. 65ff.

[11] See his article in *Vigiliae Christianae*, vol. 8, nos. 1–2 (January–April, 1954) and his book, *He Ascended into Heaven*, p. 194, n.3.

The *Apostolic Constitutions,* originating in Syria about 375–400, make a definite reference to the fortieth day:

'Count forty days from the Lord's Day to the fifth day of the week, and celebrate the feast of the Ascension of the Lord, wherein he finished all his dispensation and constitution, and returned to that God and Father that sent him, and sat down at the right hand of power, and remains there until his enemies are put under his feet.' [12]

But it is the sermons of those who preached on Ascension Day that give the most solid evidence of its observance. John Chrysostom, Bishop of Constantinople (*d.* 407), is one of the first known in the East to have delivered homilies on this festival. He referred to the feast of 'the ascension of our Lord to the heavens' in a sermon given at Antioch between 386 and 398. 'When we kept the commemoration of the Cross,' he told a congregation at the martyrium of Romanesia just outside Antioch, 'we came outside the city to observe it. And now that we are celebrating the ascension of the Crucified, a joyful and glorious day, it is once more outside the city that we celebrate it.' [13]

At about the same time, Bishop Gregory of Nyssa was preaching on an occasion which was almost certainly the feast of the Ascension:

'For while the Gospel told the story of the Lord's time and life on earth, that mighty prophet, David, so transcending himself as if no longer limited by his human abilities, and being infused with supernatural powers, utters their voices to us. . . . The mystery of the death is already fulfilled, the victory gained over the enemies, and the banner of the cross raised over against them. He has ascended again to the heights, he has taken captivity captive and given to men the life, the kingdom, and all those good gifts. He had to open once more the gates on high.' [14]

In the West Ascension Day sermons were not heard until a little later. In a homily attributed to Chromatius, Bishop of Aquileia in northern Italy (*d.* 407), the opening verses of Isaiah 63 are quoted and also Psalm 24. There is a note of insistence that the feast should be kept, as if it was an innovation. Philaster, Bishop of Brescia (*d. c.* 397) also seems to

[12] V, 19 (*Ante-Nicene Christian Library,* vol. xvii, p. 140).
[13] *Hom.* 1 (Cabié, p. 200).
[14] *In Pentecosten* (Cabié, p. 199).

have known the festival. But it is not until the time of Leo (440–61) that sermons were preached on this occasion in Rome:

'Dearly beloved, the number of the sacred forty days was fulfilled, which were ordained by divine providence, and used for the increase of sacred knowledge, so that while the time of our Lord's bodily presence among us was by him extended by this measure of time, our faith in his resurrection was strengthened by proofs closely linked one with the other. . . .

'Therefore since the Ascension of Christ is our uplifting, and whither the glory of our Head shall go thither the hope of our body is called, let us, then, rejoice exceedingly with fitting joy, and let us be glad with devout giving of thanks. For on this day, not alone are we made sure heirs of paradise, but in Christ we have already reached the heights of heaven, and obtained more abundant gifts through the ineffable fervour of Christ than we lost through the envy of the devil.' [15]

Augustine remarked in his letter to Januarius that Ascension Day was not one of the feasts laid down in scripture, though he went on to attribute to the apostles and early councils 'the observance of the yearly commemorations of the Lord's passion, his resurrection, his ascension, and the coming of the Holy Spirit. These, like others, are kept by the whole Church.' Several of his Ascension Day sermons have survived. When one of these was preached, the festival happened to fall on the same day as a local commemoration:

'(Christ) showed himself to his disciples that they might see him with their eyes and touch him with their hands, showing them what he had become, and that he had not put off what he always was. For forty days he spoke with them, as you have heard, going in and coming out, eating and drinking together with them; not now from need, but wholly from power, and making plain to them the true nature of his body: mortal upon the cross, immortal from the grave.

'This day then we are celebrating the Lord's ascension. To-day there is also a festival proper to this church: the death of the founder of this basilica of the holy Leontius. But it is fitting that the star be overshadowed by the sun. So let us, as we begin, speak rather of the Lord. . . .' [16]

[15] *Sermo.* 73 (*The Sunday Sermons of the Great Fathers*, vol. ii, ed. by M. F. Toal, p. 425).
[16] *Sermo.* 262 (Toal, op. cit., p. 415).

For Augustine, Ascension Day was—as later liturgiologists would say—'privileged'!

To sum up, it would have made this chapter very much tidier if we had been able to trace the emergence of Ascension Day in a smooth geographical and chronological movement across the Mediterranean; but the life of the Church, and especially her worship, rarely evolves in that textbook-ish kind of way. New features in the calendar had to win their acceptance by their usefulness and their popularity until councils and bishops legislated about them, and it was only because it proved useful and popular that Ascension Day came to be observed during the last decade of the fourth and the early decades of the fifth century on the fortieth day after Easter. Its effect was to make a breach in the unity of the great Fifty Days and to give the calendar a more commemorative character than it had had previously. The rise of other commemorative festivals, such as Whitsunday, added to the process.

V. Whitsunday

At the same time that Ascension Day was appearing in the calendar, the fiftieth day began to gather to itself the themes of the last of the events in the economy of salvation. We have seen that during the fourth century it was treated as a closing assembly with special stress on the ascension and *sessio* of Christ and the gift of the Holy Spirit. Later in this century it came to be regarded as a feast day commemorating the events of the first Pentecost. The consolidation of the doctrine of the Trinity and the necessity of refuting errors about the Third Person of the Godhead gave impetus to the development.

Sometimes the name 'Pentecost' was used in its newer as well as its older meaning in the same context. In a homily on Psalm 95 Gregory of Nyssa (a champion of the Spirit's divinity in the face of the Pneumatomachian heresy) said:

'The same prophet (David) illuminates for us the great feast of Pentecost, his hand striking again on the bow of the Spirit with the strings of wisdom. Let him speak now from that inspired song, suited to this moment of grace: ' "O come, let us give thanks unto the Lord." The perfect food for our human nature is here for us—the Holy Spirit, in whom is life. This is the fundamental meaning of this festival. . . . To-day, the days of Pentecost being accomplished, according to the yearly cycle of time, at this very hour, that is to say, the third hour, is given the grace which surpasses all description.' [1]

During the fifth century 'Pentecost' was used in official documents to refer to the fiftieth day for the purpose of fixing a date. A charge from the emperor Theodosius, summoning the bishops to the council of Antioch in 431 to deal with the Nestorian heresy, asked them to be there 'on the day of the holy Pentecost.' But the older tradition survived among the Fathers during much of this time. They called it 'the *Quinquagesima*' (Hilary, Bishop of Poitiers, *d.* 367), 'the seven weeks of the holy Pentecost' (Basil, Bishop of Caesarea, *d.* 379), 'the

[1] *In Pentecosten.*

whole Pentecost of fifty days' (Epiphanius, Bishop of Salamis, *d*. 403) and 'the whole course of fifty days, reckoned as Sundays' (Maximus, Bishop of Turin, *d*. 470). And, as we shall see, the pale shadow of it has never been completely lost in the Church's calendar, even down to the present day.

Western Christendom may have been a decade or two behind the Eastern Churches in accepting Ascension Day and Whitsunday as feast days, though by the time of Leo they were observed in Rome. In Africa Augustine preached on Whitsunday: 'See how the solemnity of the Pasch has reached its conclusion without losing any of its splendour! The Pasch is the beginning of grace, Pentecost is the crown!'[2]

But what made Whitsunday so important was that, like Easter, it became a baptismal day. This gave it the liturgical status of a second Pasch. Leo felt that these two days were the only fitting occasions in the year when baptism should be administered. On October 21st, 447, he wrote to the bishops in Sicily that he had been surprised to hear they had been willing to baptize more people on the feast of Epiphany than at Easter:

'My dear brethren, this is then a very far-reaching and important matter about which there can be no doubt. You know well that before baptism the candidates must, according to the apostolic rule, undergo the scrutinies of exorcism, they must be sanctified by fasting, and they must be instructed by frequent exhortations. And only two occasions must be used for this: Easter and Pentecost.'[3]

He repeated the same directions in a letter on March 6th, 459, to some bishops in central Italy who had baptized on the anniversaries of martyrdoms, 'instead of during the Paschal festival, to which only Pentecost may be compared.'

There seems to have been some resistance to the custom of baptizing on Whitsunday in the East. John Chrysostom argued that catechumens could only be prepared properly if they kept the pre-paschal fast. But the precedent of Acts 2, when three thousand were baptized on that day, was against him. Twenty years later Gregory of Nazianzus administered the sacrament on the feasts of Epiphany and Whitsunday as well as at Easter.

The numerical symbolism associated with the most joyful

[2] Quoted by E. Flicoteaux, *Le Rayonnement de la Pentecôte*, p. 53.
[3] *Epist.* XVI.

season was not forgotten, but it was readjusted to fit in with the new scheme of feasts. Peter Chrysologus (*c.* 400–50), Bishop of Ravenna, declared:

'Number forty has lifted our infirm nature to heaven; number fifty, as we see to-day, pours out the divine nature upon earth. O happy exchange, given to the Church in the currency of numerals! As scripture says, number forty ended the captivity of man by the ascension of Christ; by the coming of the Spirit number fifty restores the liberty long desired!'[4]

Similarly, there was a shift in the interpretation of pentecostal imagery, illustrating how the spiritual thought of the Church adapted itself to the liturgical changes. Formerly much had been made of the great Fifty Days as the period of harvest and the offering of first-fruits, of the mystery of seven times seven plus one, and of the 'days of the Bridegroom.' Now the preachers began to look elsewhere and use a new series of symbols to teach the meaning of Whitsunday: the new wine in the old skins, the tower of Babel, and the Law and the Spirit.

In both St. Matthew and St. Luke the saying about the Bridegroom is followed by the warning that 'new wine (is not put) into old wineskins; if it is, the skins burst, and the wine is spilled, and the skins are destroyed.'[5] And the Church turned to this as an illustration to explain what had happened when the disciples had received the Holy Spirit. The crowd in Jerusalem had thought they were drunk. In a more profound sense, this was true: they were spiritually inebriated by the gift, for the Holy Spirit had come to them as 'wine that maketh glad the heart of man' (Psalm 104). So, too, all Christians who receive the Holy Spirit are 'renewed in the spirit of (their) minds and (have) put on the new nature, created after the likeness of God in true righteousness and holiness.'[6]

This theme was elaborated in a homily by Gregory of Nyssa for Whitsunday in a typically colourful way:

'Then do the enemies of the Spirit's glory see that the fiery tongue of the divine words has enlightened what has been hidden? Shall they make fun of those who speak as if filled with new wine? Although they criticize us in this way, for my

[4] *Sermo.* XI.
[5] Matthew 9:17 = Luke 5:37.
[6] Ephesians 4:23–4.

part, my brothers, I urge you not to fear the insults of such people and not to be depressed by their evil talk. Indeed, may they come to accept for themselves this new wine, this sweet wine, that flows from the winepress on which the Lord treads in the Gospel, to make his own grapes (his blood!) as a drink for you! May they also come to be filled with the new wine, the sweet wine, which has not been spoilt by publicans diluting it with the water of heresy! May they come to be filled by the Spirit entirely, through whom those who live in him expurgate the scum and slime of unbelief! Yet such people cannot accept the new wine for themselves while they carry round the old skin which, being unable to contain such wine, breaks into heresy. But as for us, my brothers, "Come," as the prophet says, "let us give thanks unto the Lord," drinking the sweetness of true religion, as Esdras commanded. Enlightened by the chorus of apostles and prophets, let us rejoice in the gift of the Holy Spirit and exalt on this day that the Lord has made, in Christ.' [7]

Augustine used the same symbolism, but in a more restrained manner:

'As it was the Lord's resurrection which confirmed men in the faith of his divinity, who deigned to become man for us, so after his ascension into heaven they are even more confirmed by the fullest and most perfect gift of the Holy Spirit, whom he sent. From that time they became as new skins able to receive new wine. That is why, when they spoke in tongues, they were said to be drunk and full of new wine. The voice of the Lord in scripture witnesses to those who will hear: "No one puts new wine in old wineskins," said the Lord. So new wine was put into new skins. For the old skins are such as think of Christ after the flesh—like the apostle Peter when the Lord said to him, "Get thee behind me, Satan: thou art a stumbling block to me," because he believed Christ would not die and perish in the same way as other men.' [8]

A sermon by an unknown Western author of about this period pictured the fermentation of the new wine as a means of purification. He based it on a verse from Psalm 104:

'While many marvelled at so great a mystery, others mocked and said, "They are filled with new wine." Unknowingly they spoke the truth, because in the fermentation of new

[7] *In Pentecosten.*
[8] *Sermo Mai* 156.

51

wine, all impurities are banished so that it may protect its bouquet and keep its taste. The new wineskins received new wine, conserving it; thus the apostles walked in the newness of the Holy Spirit. The prophet spoke of the Holy Spirit when he said, "When thou lettest thy breath go forth they shall be made: and thou shalt renew the face of the earth." The face of the earth has been truly renewed and cultivated, when the voice of thanksgiving sings praises to the heavenly power and intones hymns to God.' [9]

Almost without exception, the Fathers understood the gift of tongues to mean the miraculous ability to speak foreign languages without previous study or preparation in order that the Church could preach the Gospel to all the nations, and it prompted them to see in Pentecost a reversal of the disobedience at Babel. It was indeed a wonderful miracle, commented Gregory of Nazianzus, for through the work of the one Spirit each man had found unity in understanding what God had done.[10]

From the tower of Babel the Fathers drew a lesson in the Church's catholicity: the evil that had formerly divided men had been overthrown in the triumph of Christ. This was John Chrysostom's motif when he preached on Whitsunday in Antioch:

'In former times men, seized by madness, wanted to build a tower to reach to heaven; but he (the Lord), by dividing their tongues, divided their evil agreement. So now the Holy Spirit swoops upon them in fiery tongues to unify a divided world. The result is something new and strange. For as in former times tongues had divided men and frustrated their wicked intention, so now tongues united the world and converted discord into harmony.' [11]

Augustine said that descendants of Noah had presumed to try to reach the heavens through their own efforts and so they had brought down upon themselves the wrath of God, he explained. To restore the harmony that had been broken, humility was necessary—a humility that enabled men to await salvation as the free gift of God. The gift of the Spirit came

9 Cabié, p. 227.

10 The lesson is not necessarily lost, however, if we take the gift of tongues to mean that charism which accompanies and fosters prayer and praise of God—the more usual interpretation of glossolalia nowadays.

11 Hom. II de sacra Pentecoste.

upon those who were united in the Body of Christ by faith and baptism: this is why Peter replied to the people who asked him what they must do, ' "Repent and be baptized every one of you in the name of Jesus Christ for the remission of your sins and you will receive the gift of the Holy Spirit." ' Babel represents the wicked city, 'Babylon the great, which hath made all the nations drink of the wine of wrath.' Her fall is a prelude to the triumph of the new Jerusalem, coming down from heaven 'as a bride adorned for her husband.'

For Augustine, Pentecost meant joining in the victory of the new Jerusalem, living in the Church of the paschal mystery:

'The man who has the Holy Spirit is in the Church, and the Church speaks the languages of all. Whoever is outside this Church does not have the Holy Spirit. For the Holy Spirit deigned to reveal himself in the languages of all peoples, in order that he who remains in the church's unity, which speaks all languages, might know that he has the Holy Spirit. There is one body, said the apostle Paul, one body and one spirit. Look at the members of your body. The body consists of many members, and one spirit inspires them all. . . . What our spirit—that is to say, our soul—is to our members, so is the Holy Spirit to the members of Christ, the Body of Christ, the Church.'

So the significance of the feast came to centre on the Church herself and her nature as a Spirit-filled society in Christ.

'And now, my brothers,' said Augustine, 'members of the Body of Christ, seeds of unity, sons of peace, keep this day in rejoicing, celebrate in security. For in you is fulfilled that which was prefigured in these days when the Holy Spirit came.' [12]

An old collect, which is found in the Leonine, Gelasian, and Gregorian sacramentaries, sums it up neatly:

'Almighty and eternal God, who has willed that the paschal sacrament may be continued in the mystery of fifty days, make the peoples dispersed by the division of languages to be joined by your heavenly gift in the united praise of your name.'

The circumstances in which the Holy Spirit was given to the disciples in the upper room also led the Fathers to see in

[12] *Sermo*. 268.

Whitsunday a fulfilment of the Jewish Pentecost with its commemoration of the giving of the Law. The descent of the Holy Spirit in tongues of fire sealed the new Israel under the new covenant just as the glory of God on the mountain had sealed the old Israel under the Mosaic covenant. Leo pointed out that both were the work of the same Holy Spirit:

'For as, fifty days after the immolation of the paschal lamb, the Law was given on mount Sinai to the Hebrews, freed from the Egyptian bondage, so after the passion of Christ, put to death as the true Lamb of God, the Holy Spirit fell upon the apostles and the group of believers fifty days after his resurrection. Thus the watchful Christian easily recognizes that the initiation of the old covenant laid the foundations of the Gospel, and that the second covenant was established by the same Spirit who instituted the first.' [13]

Augustine interpreted the finger that wrote on the tablets of stone as a symbol of the Holy Spirit. He compared two passages from the synoptic gospels, 'If I by the Spirit of God cast out devils. . . . If I by the finger of God cast out devils . . .' and went on to quote Paul, 'Ye are an epistle of Christ, ministered by us, written not with ink, but with the Spirit of the living God; not in tables of stone, but in tables that are hearts of flesh.'

'So we keep Pentecost,' he wrote, 'that is, the fiftieth day after the passion and resurrection of the Lord, for then he sent us the Holy Spirit, the Paraclete, as he had promised. The Pasch of the Jews signified what would happen, for fifty days after the observance of the lamb that was slain, Moses received on the mountain the Law written by the finger of God.' [14]

John Chrysostom put it this way: 'The apostles did not descend from the mountain carrying tables of stone in their hands like Moses, but bearing the Holy Spirit in their hearts. And, with charisms and all kind of blessings flooding out of a treasury and fountain of knowledge, they went everywhere, having become by grace living scriptures and living commandments.' [15]

Judging by the references to it in the fifth century, Whit-

[13] *De Pentecostes* I.
[14] Matthew 12:28; Luke 11:20; 2 Corinthians 3:3; *Sermo Mai* 158; *Contra Faustum* 32.
[15] *In Matthaeum Hom. I.*

sunday was by then a well established festival. An unknown preacher in northern Italy said:

'It is ten days since we celebrated the ascension of Christ the Lord: to-day we celebrate the mystery of the Holy Spirit's visitation. This glorious day is the fiftieth after the Lord's resurrection: it is the day when the Spirit of God poured out the flames of his love.' [16]

After mentioning the Law-giving on Sinai, the preacher went on to discuss the fruits of the mystery celebrated on that day—the unity of men in the divine love and the renewal of all things as prophesied in Psalm 104 ('When thou lettest thy breath go forth they shall be made: and thou shalt renew the face of the earth').

Some of the first pentecostal hymns are dated from this century. The response *Advenit ignis divinus* sung in the Roman office of matins in the week after Whitsunday may have originated in this period: 'Come, divine fire, not burning but inspiring, not consuming but enlightening, and enter the hearts of the disciples giving to them gifts of grace. . . .' Paulinus, Bishop of Nola (353–431) wrote a hymn about 'this solemn day on which the Holy Spirit, sent from heaven on high, divided tongues in fiery light. . . .'

Another anonymous homily indicates that a series of lections had just been read to the congregation: the jubilee of the fiftieth year (Lev. 25), the canticle of the vineyard ('Let me sing for my beloved a love song concerning his vineyard,' Isa. 5), the appearances of the angel of the Lord to Balaam, Joshua and Gideon (Num. 22; Joshua 5; Judges 6), the theophany on Sinai (Exod. 19) and the gift of the Holy Spirit (Acts 2). The gospel lection was probably taken from John 14–15. It seems almost certain that this was preached on Whitsunday, possibly after the vigil at the beginning of the mass.

A Whitsun sermon attributed to Faustus, Bishop of Riez (*c.* 408–*c.* 490) was used by the schoolmen in the early Middle Ages because it touched on the relationship between baptism and confirmation:

'In these days, the Lord said, "I will pour out my Spirit on all flesh." Let us watch for the riches of the goodness on high: what each of the neophytes now come to receive by the laying on of hands in confirmation, the descent of the Holy

[16] Cabié, p. 211.

55

Spirit on the gathering of the faithful then gave to all. . . .
Perhaps someone may ask, "What good can it do me, after
the mystery of baptism, to receive the ministry of confirmation?" . . . In baptism we are born again, after baptism we are
confirmed for the fight; in baptism we are washed, after
baptism we are strengthened.' [17]

This sermon may have been preached during the Whitsun
vigil when the catechumens were receiving baptism and confirmation in preparation for their first communion. By the
end of the fifth century this vigil was kept in the Church
at Tours—Bishop Perpetuus (461–91) is credited with having
introduced it—and at the beginning of the following century
it was observed in Arles. Bishop Caesarius (c. 470–542) told
the congregation at the end of matins on Whitsunday morning
that he did not intend to preach for very long as they must be
tired after keeping the vigil!

[17] Quoted in J. D. C. Fisher, *Christian Initiation: Baptism in the
Medieval West*, p. 144.

VI. *Octaves, Fasts and Litanies*

As festivals of a historical-commemorative type, Ascension Day and Whitsunday broke up the unity of the ancient Pentecost. In the development of the Christian calendar from the fourth century onwards, other observances appeared in association with the great Fifty Days to continue this breaking-up process, and it is these that we must now examine.

(1) *The Easter Octave*

The practice of enhancing major feasts by extending their celebration over an eight-day period was probably inspired by Old Testament precedents. There were octaves connected with Jewish feasts like Passover-Unleavened Bread, Tabernacles, and the Dedication of the Temple because, as we have seen, eight days had a particularly symbolic value in Hebrew thought.

It appears that the dedication of the Constantinian basilicas in Jerusalem and Tyre occupied eight days. The earliest reference to an Easter octave occurs in the *Codex Theodosianus*. Theodosius II, who was emperor from 408 to 435, set up a commission to codify all the ordinances that had been enacted since Constantine and to bring them up-to-date, and one of the sources—probably laid down in 389 by the emperor Valentinian II—orders that the law courts are to be closed during the week before and the week after Easter, fifteen days in all. It shows that considerable importance was attached in the Christian Empire to the observance of Holy Week and Easter Week.

By this time it was customary for the newly-baptized to go to church daily during Easter week for mass and for further instruction. The old liturgies of Milan, Gaul and Spain have two masses for each of the days within the octave, one for the ordinary congregation and one *pro baptizatis*. Ambrose of Milan, Cyril of Jerusalem, John Chrysostom, Theodore of Mopsuesta and Augustine of Hippo all used to preach to the neophytes during the week. The latter told his *infantes* that they were 'tender shoots of holiness, born again of water and of the Holy Spirit, planted and watered by us in the field of God, who gives the increase.'

During her pilgrimage Egeria noted that the week was kept in Jerusalem: 'The paschal days are kept up to a late hour, as with us, and the services take place in their order throughout the eight paschal days, as it is the custom everywhere at Easter throughout the octave.' She went on to describe how the bishop went up to Eleona and to Imbomon after breakfast with all the clergy and people on these days to sing hymns and recite prayers.

At first the octave ended on the Saturday after Easter in Rome—the eight days were calculated from the vigil on Holy Saturday—but gradually it was stretched until Low Sunday came to be regarded as the eighth day. Across the Mediterranean in Hippo, Augustine evidently thought of Low Sunday as the end of the octave for in his sermon on that day he said, 'To-day is for us a day of unending joy within a great mystery.' Then he went on to warn his listeners of the dangers of being too much taken up with secular affairs when the courts reopened: 'The festival days are now at an end and are followed by days of contracts, of actions against debtors, of disputes. Be careful how you pass your life among such things. The quiet of these days should inspire you to an inner peace, not to thoughts of quarrels.' [1] Evidently the excitement and scandal of the legal processes played an absorbing part in the lives of ordinary citizens!

The octave was established as a liturgical observance when each day acquired its own mass—it was almost completed when the Gelasian Sacramentary was in use—and the effect was to give Easter week the nature of a little paschaltide within the greater Paschaltide: the fifty days' rejoicing was focused on the first eight days and narrowed to a celebration of Christ's resurrection and of the baptismal resurrection of Christians.

(2) The Rogations

The *Litaniae minores* (Rogations) were instituted by Mamertus (*d. c.* 475), Bishop of Vienne in Gaul, when his diocese was stricken by volcanic eruptions. Avitus, who was consecrated to the see about 490, described how they were fixed:

[1] *Sermo.* 259 (Toal, op. cit., p. 280).

'Bishop Mamertus, my predecessor and spiritual father since my baptism, himself conceived the idea of the Rogations during the holy vigil of Easter, and he worked out before God the scheme of psalms and prayers used everywhere to-day. . . . The present time of three days between the previous Sunday and the holy Ascension was chosen because the period seemed particularly suitable for these observances. In the following years certain churches among the Gauls copied the excellent example, though not always keeping the Rogations on the same days that they had first been fixed among us. However, the bishops were filled with admiration for the Rogations, and in time they were kept everywhere on the same date, that is, on the days we now have them.' [2]

It is a warning of the dangers of individual liturgical experiments! Being penitential in character, the Rogations conflicted with the spirit of the great Fifty Days. But by now the unity of Eastertide was completely forgotten. In a surprisingly short time the Council of Orleans (511) was legislating in such a way that one would think they were concerned with an ancient observance:

'All Churches must keep the Rogations, that is, the Litanies, before Ascension Day so that the three daily fasts are completed before the festival itself. During these three days, all serfs and servants must be freed from work so that a great crowd can assemble from everywhere. During these three days, every one must fast and eat Lenten food.'

By the seventh and eighth centuries formularies appear in the service books for the Rogations. A book of the gospels in Milan has a passage from Matt. 15 ('I have pity on the crowd for they have now been with me three days') as a reading on the third and final Rogation Day; the epistle and gospel in the Roman missal are also very old (Jas. 5: 16–20, 'Elijah prayed earnestly,' and Luke 11: 5–13, the parable of the friend at midnight). Perhaps they are the very passages which came into Mamertus' mind as he kept that Easter vigil at the end of the fifth century.

The name *Litaniae minores* was given to the Rogations to distinguish them from the Greater Litanies, which began to be kept in Rome on April 25th from the sixth century onwards. The origin of the *Litaniae majores* is obscure: they may have been a christianized version of a secular observance. Although

[2] *Hom. in Rogationibus.*

they fell within the great Fifty Days, the processions connected with the Greater Litanies did not conflict with the joyful character of the season for they were not intended to be penitential.

(3) *The Resumption of the Fast after Ascension Day*

When the fortieth day was kept as the festival of Christ's return to heaven, it no longer seemed logical to regard the following ten days as among the number of the 'days of the Bridegroom.' 'He spent forty days with them (the disciples),' said Augustine. 'The Bridegroom, as he was about to leave, entrusted his Bride to his friends.' Some adjustment of the older interpretation was necessary. The Bridegroom was *absent*, it was argued, therefore the Church must fast!

The practice of resuming the fast after Ascension Day was familiar to John Cassian when he visited the Egyptian monastic establishments over the turn of the fourth and the fifth centuries, for in his *Conferences*, written in Gaul some years later, he describes how he and his friend put a question about it to Abba Theonas, 'Why do you relax the rigour of your abstinence at meals all through the fifty days, whereas Christ only remained with his disciples forty days after his resurrection?' The Abba's reply shows that his community was faithful to the more primitive tradition regarding the discipline of Pentecost:

'The apostles waited ten days. When these were fulfilled on the fiftieth day they received him with joy. And thus in this way the number of their festival was clearly made up, which, as we read, was figuratively foreshadowed also in the Old Testament, for when seven weeks were fulfilled the bread of the firstfruits was ordered to be offered by the priests to the Lord: and this was indeed shown to be offered to the Lord by the preaching of the apostles, which they are said on that day to have addressed to the people; the true bread of the firstfruits, which when produced from the instruction of the new doctrine, consecrated the firstfruits of the Jews as a Christian people to the Lord, five thousand men being filled with the gifts of the food. And therefore these ten days are kept with equal solemnity and joy as the previous forty. And the tradition about this festival, transmitted to us by apostolic men, should be kept with the same uniformity. For therefore on those days they do not bow their knees in prayer, because the bending of the knees is a sign of penitence and mourning. Wherefore also during these days we observe in all things the same solemnities as on Sunday, on which day our predecessors taught that men ought not to fast nor to bow the knee, out of reverence for the Lord's resurrection.'[3]

But the implication of the newer calendar was irresistible. Isidore (c. 560–636), Bishop of Seville, said that the Church should fast after Ascension Day in preparation for the gift of the Spirit; these were the days, he said, which Christ referred to when he said the disciples should fast when the Bridegroom was taken from them:

'When the time came for Christ to ascend into heaven, taking from us his physical presence, the fast indicates that through lowliness of heart and abstinence from meat we might be worthy to receive from heaven the promised Holy Spirit.'[4]

(4) *Ember Days and the Whitsun Octave*

For a long time the seasonal fasts known as Embertides (*Quattuor tempora*) were peculiar to the Roman Church. They spread gradually as the Roman rite became the normal use in other parts of Christendom—to Naples and England in the seventh century, to Gaul in the eighth, and to Spain and Milan in the eleventh and twelfth. When they first began it is impossible to say. Even in Leo's time they were regarded as ancient institutions. (He certainly approved of them: 'After these days of holy gladness . . . a fast is ordered as a healthy and necessary exercise, so that if any undue licence has broken out through neglect or indiscipline during the joys of the festival, it may be corrected by the remedy of abstinence.'[5])

The weekly fasts of the Christian community on Wednesdays and Fridays go back to primitive times. The *Liber pontificalis* attributes to Callistus, Bishop of Rome (217–22), the ordering of a Saturday fast on three occasions each year at the time of the corn, wine and oil harvests (in deference to Zechariah 8: 19). If Saturday was kept as a fast as well as a Wednesday and a Friday during a week in the months of

[3] *Conferences* xxi, 2 (*Nicene and Post-Nicene Fathers*, p. 507). It is possible that Cassian's description reflects the customs of the Church in southern Gaul, where he established himself about 410.

[4] *De eccl. off.* xxxviii (Cabié, p. 247).

[5] *Sermo.* LXXVIII (*Nicene and Post-Nicene Fathers*, vol. xii, p. 193).

June, September and December, then this may well have been the origin of the Embertides—the Lenten Ember Days could have been added later.

The Ember Days in Whit week, therefore, are very much older than the octave which came to be attached to the festival of the Holy Spirit. Consequently they tended to conflict with its festal character. The process by which they were at first dislodged and then put back into the week can be followed in various service books and lectionaries. The Gelasian Sacramentary, which is dated about the eighth century but which contains material from the Roman Church of two hundred years previously, has no masses for Whit week except the three Ember Days. The preface for the Wednesday tells the congregation that they have now entered a period of fasting 'after these days of great joy.' Gradually their formularies were moved beyond what is now Trinity Sunday as the masses for all the days in the Whitsun octave were provided, but in the end they returned to their old position. The reason was that Ember Days had become associated with the ordination Sundays, and since the Sunday after Whitsun was by tradition an important ordination day, the Ember Days became firmly rooted within the Whitsun octave.[6] As we shall see, a kind of compromise was reached in retaining or removing either the Whitsun or the Embertide lections and chants.

To complete the story of the Whitsun octave, we should add that a mass in honour of the Blessed Trinity appeared in the works of Alcuin, the great English scholar who became adviser to Charlemagne (c. 735–804). Soon afterwards this mass was assigned to the first Sunday after Whitsunday as a kind of summary of all that had been done for man as commemorated in the calendar since Christmas by God the Father, God the Son, and God the Holy Spirit. It was opposed by some bishops on the grounds that every Sunday was a Sunday in honour of the Blessed Trinity, but eventually it was accepted by the Church as a whole. The day was especially popular in England, perhaps because it was associated with Thomas Becket, who was consecrated bishop on that Sunday. In the Sarum missal and in the rites of the Carmelite and Dominican orders the remainder of the Sundays in the year are numbered after Trinity Sunday—a custom which has survived in the Book of Common Prayer. The Roman missal

[6] G. G. Willis, *Essays in Early Roman Liturgy,* pp. 68–72.

retains the older tradition of numbering these days as Sundays 'after Pentecost.'

*　　*　　*

With the emergence of these festivals, their octaves, the fasts and the litanies, the 'Great Sunday' had all but vanished. Yet not quite. Although the lections and chants of the Roman missal are drawn from a time when the evolution was nearly completed, traces of the older season still remain. Before we continue with a closer examination of the missal, therefore, we will briefly list where these traces are to be found.

(1) *'Eastertide'*

Although the establishment of the Whitsun octave pushed the paschal period back to the Saturday after Whitsunday, adding a further seven to the great Fifty Days, the name 'Eastertide' is virtually a later version of the older title, 'Pentecost.' The Roman Missal still has a rubric after the mass for the Saturday in Whit week, *Post missam expirat tempus paschali.* The rule about standing for prayer remains in the Roman Breviary which has a note saying, 'There are no genuflections during the whole of Eastertide.'

(2) *'Alleluia'*

Although 'Alleluia' is nowadays sung at other times, its use by ancient custom is particularly attached to the great Fifty Days in the West. The Roman missal lays down that it shall be used when certain saints' days fall within the season. Augustine described its purpose as follows:

'The time of mourning which is signified by the forty days (Lent) is to us both a sign and its realization. As for the time of rejoicing, rest and divine rule, signified by these days (Eastertide), we have a sign for it in the "Alleluia," though we do not yet have its realization in praise. Still, we say in hope, "Alleluia." But what is "Alleluia"? "Praise the Lord!" That is why in these days after the resurrection, the praises of God are made more frequently in church, because after our own resurrection we shall become a perpetual praise.' [7]

There is a story that when Germanus, Bishop of Auxerre, came to Britain, he ministered to the Saxon army during the

[7] *Sermo.* 254.

Lent of 430. On the night of holy Saturday he baptized a great number of soldiers with water from the River Alen in Flintshire. Just as the Easter mass had finished, the bishop heard that the Picts were approaching, so he posted the newly-baptized soldiers in the hills overlooking the valley along which the enemy would come. As the invaders came up, the Christian soldiers raised a great shout of 'Alleluia! ' which was taken up by others to echo round the hills. The Picts imagined that an immense army was about to attack them and they fled. A victory had been won without a blow being struck. Whatever else this story reveals, it shows that the 'Alleluia' was a cry of triumph appropriate for the Church in Eastertide.[8]

(3) 'Mid-Pentecost'

At one time the Wednesday after the third Sunday in Eastertide was known as 'Mid-Pentecost.' References to it appear in the late fourth and fifth centuries in Asia Minor, Syria, and some parts of the West. With it was associated the pericope from John 14, 'About *the middle of the feast*, Jesus went up into the temple and taught. . . .' There is no trace of this old name to-day, but oddly enough the reading from St. John now appears as the gospel for the Tuesday after mid-Lent (Lent IV) in the Roman missal.

(4) *The Lections from St. John, Acts and the Book of Revelation*

The study of comparative liturgy shows that the Church has traditionally reserved for Eastertide the reading of certain books in the Bible—St. John's Gospel, the Acts of the Apostles, and the Book of Revelation.

In the Byzantine liturgy, which has only two readings at the eucharist, the choice is very clear: the lections begin with Acts 1 and John 1 on Easter Day and they are taken from these same books for the other Sundays in Eastertide. The Ambrosian liturgy has three lections, two of which are nearly always taken from Acts and St. John. The Gallican and Spanish liturgies have lections from Revelation and Acts. The Roman rite, as we shall see, also has readings from St. John on the Sundays after Easter, but its pericopes from

---

[8] A column called the Alleluia monument is situated in a place named Maes Garmon—the field of Germanus—about a mile to the west of Mold.

Acts are limited to the masses of the Easter octave. Lections from Revelation are set for the masses for martyrs in Eastertide.

The nature of these three books is particularly suitable to all that the great Fifty Days signified: St. John's Gospel is illuminated from the beginning with Jesus Christ as the Word and the Lamb of God, 'full of grace and truth,' and the promise and power of the Holy Spirit; Acts pictures the Church advancing in the triumph of the resurrection and under the direct and dynamic leadership of the Holy Spirit; the Apocalypse unfolds the secret plan of God, a plan that will make a reality on earth the announcement that 'the sovereignty of the world has passed to our Lord and his Christ, and he shall reign for ever and ever.' [9]

[9] Revelation 11:15. See the Appendix A, p. 99.

E

VII. *From Easter Day to Low Sunday*

The lections and chants provided in the Roman missal for the great Fifty Days are a product of the evolution we have been following in this book. The seeds scattered in the early centuries of Christian teaching and devotion have grown and blossomed into an untidy but fascinating centrepiece in the garden of the liturgical year. Since any revision of the calendar in the West must take into account how and why these lections and chants were chosen (they are the basis for the epistles and gospels of the Sundays in Eastertide in the Book of Common Prayer and its successors) we will examine them in this and the following chapter, trying to trace such patterns and themes as are still discernible.

At one time there was no prescribed lectionary for the readings at mass. The deacon or lector read from the scriptures until instructed by the presiding bishop to stop. In this way the various books of the Bible were read through continuously (*lectio continua*). Many of the early sermons show that they were simply commentaries on passages that had just been read. One of Augustine's sermons (No. 341) seems to suggest that there had been three lections, one from the Old Testament, one from the Epistles and one from the Gospels in the service over which he was presiding; but on another occasion (No. 176) he referred to an epistle, a psalm and a gospel, presumably two readings and a chant in between. There were three lections in Rome during the fifth and sixth centuries, but the Old Testament reading was eventually dropped. It survives in the Roman missal only on certain days, such as the Wednesday in the fourth week of Lent, the Wednesday in Holy Week, and Good Friday. (The Old Testament lections which the missal provides for occasions like the Saturdays in Embertide are not, strictly speaking, readings at mass but the remains of ancient vigil services.)

The earliest lectionaries, which preserve the usage of the seventh and eighth centuries, show that pericopes from the scriptures were being assigned to particular days and seasons, and it is in this period that the present lections came to be established. The readings for Eastertide were, in fact, some of the first to be set.

Besides the lections, the Roman missal provides for all its masses throughout the year verses of biblical and occasionally non-biblical material in the introit with its antiphon (*antiphona ad introitum*), the gradual, the alleluia and its verse, the tract, the offertory (*antiphona ad offertorium*), and the communion (*communio*). These are chants sung at various stages during mass: the introit at the entrance of the clergy, the gradual, the alleluia and its verse, and/or the tract between the epistle and the gospel, the offertory at the preparation of the altar, and the communion during the administration of the sacrament.

At one time they were very much longer than they are now. A whole psalm was sung during the entrance of the clergy. This was necessary because the earliest arrangement in the Roman basilicas placed the sacristry near the door of the church at the opposite end to the apse. When sacristries were built nearer the sanctuary, the entrance of the clergy took less time and so fewer verses were needed. All that remains of this introit psalm is one verse, usually the first, with its antiphon and *Gloria Patri*.[1]

The way in which the chants were sung has had an effect on the way their relics have remained in the missal. The introit was sung antiphonally by the *schola cantorum*, the verses being divided between two groups of singers; the gradual, on the other hand, was sung in a responsorial fashion, with a cantor singing the main part of the chant and the choir and congregation replying with an unvarying response. The old name for the gradual is *responsorium graduale*: it was sung from the step (*gradus*) of the pulpit or ambo used for the lections. Like the introits, the graduals were also shortened, but because they were sung responsorially rather than anti-

[1] J. A. Jungmann, *The Mass of the Roman Rite*, p. 216. Fr. Jungmann points out that this has sometimes obscured the connection between the psalm and the day on which it is sung. On the feast of the Epiphany, for example, the first verse of Psalm 72 is sung at the introit: 'Give the King thy judgements, O God: and thy righteousness unto the King's Son.' But this psalm was originally chosen for this feast because of its tenth verse: 'The kings of Tharsis and of the isles shall give presents: the kings of Arabia and Saba shall bring gifts.'

phonally, they have survived in a different form—without antiphons and without the *Gloria Patri.*

The gradual for Easter Day was once the whole of Psalm 118 and the response was verse 24: 'This is the day which the Lord hath made: we will rejoice and be glad in it.' When the gradual was shortened and masses were provided for the days in the Easter octave, the various verses were distributed throughout the week:

Easter Day:
'O give thanks unto the Lord, for he is gracious: and his mercy endureth for ever' (verse 1).

Monday:
'Let Israel now confess that he is gracious: and his mercy endureth for ever' (verse 2).

Wednesday:
'The right hand of the Lord bringeth mighty things to pass: the right hand of the Lord hath the pre-eminence' (verses 15–16).

Thursday:
'The same stone which the builders refused: is become the headstone of the corner' (verse 22).

Friday:
'Blessed is he that cometh in the name of the Lord: God is the Lord who hath shown us light' (verses 26–7).[2]

On certain days the gradual is accompanied by the alleluia and its verse. This happens on Easter Day and throughout the octave until Saturday (the duration of the old octave). During the Sundays in Eastertide, however, there is no gradual. Instead, the alleluia is sung four times and given two verses. It is probable that the graduals and the alleluias with their verses were formerly chants at the end of different lections before the gospel when there were more than one. In the Ambrosian missal, for instance, the *psalmellus,* which cor-

[2] The quotations from the Roman rite in this and the following chapter are taken from the *English Missal.* I have not given all the scriptural references, and in most cases I have reduced the number of alleluias which, in reading a chapter like this, can get rather wearisome!

responds to the gradual in the Roman missal, is sung before the epistle and the alleluia after it.

The alleluia first appears in what is almost certainly a liturgical context in Revelation 19: 1-7 ('I heard a great voice of much people in heaven, saying, Alleluia; salvation, and glory, and honour, and power, unto the Lord our God . . .'). It is a shout of triumph taken up by the choir of heaven and by the vast throng of martyrs because God has through them broken down the last resistance to his universal reign. 'Praise the Lord!' From New Testament times it passed into the worship of the Church and it was Sozomon, a visitor to Rome from Eastern Christendom during the fifth century, who noticed that it was sung there only on Easter Day. In the following century its use was extended, first throughout Eastertide and then to all Sundays in the year except those within the penitential seasons.

During the great Fifty Days the tract only appears in the vigil of Pentecost. At one time this chant also consisted of a whole psalm, sung through without any responses (*tractim* means 'straight through'). Its use may have been limited to vigils and penitential days and seasons because of the simplicity of its musical setting.

Offertory chants were used in north Africa when Augustine was Bishop of Hippo and not long afterwards they appeared in Rome. Since offertory processions tended to be rather lengthy affairs with the congregation taking part, the responsorial method of singing its chant was employed as this occupied more time (there were no organs to be played during the awkward gaps!). Only rarely do the texts of the offertory chants mention the liturgical action they accompanied—the offertory for Whitsunday is an exception: 'For thy temple's sake at Jerusalem shall kings bring presents unto thee.' Usually they reflect the character of the season or the festival.

The communion chant is also very ancient. At one time it may have been invariable in some parts of the Church, for Jerome says, 'Each day when we are filled with heavenly bread, we say, "O taste and see how gracious the Lord is." ' All that remains of this chant is its antiphon.

A feature of Eastertide in the Roman missal are the two sequences, 'Christians, to the paschal victim offer your thankful praises' (*Victimae paschali*), used from Easter Day to the following Saturday, and 'Come, thou Holy Spirit, come' (*Veni*

Sancte Spiritus), sung from Whitsunday to the following Saturday. These are medieval additions, the former being attributed to Wipo (*d. c.* 1050), a hymn-writer of Burgundy, and the latter to Stephen Langton, Archbishop of Canterbury (*d.* 1050). A number of these sequences (the name refers to the 'following' kind of melody to which they were sung) were popular in the middle ages, but only these two together with *Lauda Sion* and *Dies ira* were retained when the missal was revised in 1570. It is thought that *Victimae paschali* may have been composed for the procession of the sacrament from the 'sepulchre' to the high altar before the Easter mass. The remains of these Easter sepulchres can sometimes be seen in our older churches. The ceremonies connected with them have long since fallen into disuse, except in some parts of Poland and central Europe.

The oldest mass of Easter Day is that printed at the end of the vigil. During the night the *electi* were prepared for their initiation into the Church and then, when they had been baptized and confirmed, they received their first Communion at this mass.

So the epistle urges them, as those who are now 'risen with Christ,' to 'seek those things which are above, where Christ sitteth on the right hand of God. . . . For ye are dead, and your life is hid with Christ in God. When Christ, who is our life, shall appear, then shall ye also appear with him in glory.' And where are they to meet him? The gospel brings the angel's message to the women at the tomb: the disciples are to meet the risen Lord in Galilee. The newly-baptized join with the choir and congregation in the three-fold alleluia and then sing: 'O give thanks unto the Lord, for he is gracious: because his mercy endureth for ever. . . . O praise the Lord, all ye heathen: praise him, all ye nations. For his merciful kindness is ever more and more towards us: and the truth of the Lord endureth for ever.'

The proper preface announces that 'Christ our Passover is sacrificed, for he is the very Lamb which hath taken away the sins of the world, who by his death hath destroyed death, and by his rising again hath restored to us life.' At one time it went on: 'Wherefore with exceeding great joy the whole round world exulteth.' Have we here an echo from the time when this mass was the liturgical entrance to the *laetissimum spatium*? Possibly, but the last sentence of this proper preface was eventually transferred to Whitsunday.

When the number of adult candidates for baptism declined, the Easter vigil was put forward earlier on Easter eve until it became necessary to provide another mass for Easter Day itself. This now appears as the mass of Easter. The epistle is 1 Cor. 5: 7-8, 'Purge out therefore the old leaven, that ye may be a new lump, as ye are unleavened. For even Christ our passover is sacrificed for us: therefore let us keep the feast, not with the old leaven, neither with the leaven of malice and wickedness; but with the unleavened bread of sincerity and truth.' The gospel is a repetition of the lection of the Easter vigil mass, but in its Marcan instead of its Matthean version.

In the introit and its antiphon we hear the voice of the risen Christ: 'I am risen, and am still with thee, alleluia: thou hast laid thine hand upon me: thy knowledge is too wonderful. O Lord, thou hast searched me out and known me: thou knowest my down-sitting, and mine uprising.' The news of the resurrection is proclaimed in the sequence, in the gospel telling of the women's discovery of the empty tomb, and in the offertory: 'The earth trembled and was still, when God arose to judgement.' As the congregation receives Communion the choir sing the verses from the epistle: 'Christ our passover is sacrificed for us: therefore let us keep the feast with the unleavened bread of sincerity and truth.' The eucharistic banquet enables Christians to participate in the mystery of Christ's death and resurrection: the way has been 'opened for us' (collect) and we pray in the secret that 'those things which we have begun in these paschal mysteries may, by thine operation, be profitable for our healing in eternity.'

During the Easter octave the Pope used to go to different stational churches each day to celebrate mass. The stational churches were the twenty-five titles served by priests under the Bishop of Rome, and the custom of holding papal masses in them served to demonstrate the unity of the Church in that city. During the week the people gathered at each station, accompanied by the neophytes wearing their baptismal robes, changing the city into what Mme. Denis-Boulet calls 'a huge walking monastery.' [3] The missal still carries the notices of these stational churches for a particular day: on Easter Day it is the great basilica of St. Mary (S. Maria Maggiore).

Between the time of Pope Gregory (d. 604) and the earliest

[3] *The Christian Calendar*, p. 175.

71

known lectionaries, the pericopes for the masses have been moved about from one day to another until they became settled in their present positions. We shall have to note the effect of this in one or two cases. Low Sunday, for example, now has the gospel that originally belonged to the day before, the old octave day. When the octave was extended to Low Sunday, the Saturday's gospel lection, John 20: 19-31 (which appropriately included the words, 'And after *eight days* . . .') was transferred to it and also its title (*Dominica*) *in deponendis albis* ('laying aside white robes').

The formularies for the masses during this octave have two themes: the resurrection of Christ and the baptism of Christians.

The resurrection theme is found mainly in the lections. Since on Monday the stational church was the basilica which Constantine had built over the traditional tomb of Peter, the gospel for the day announced that 'the Lord is risen indeed and hath appeared unto Simon,' and the news is repeated in the communion sentence. The epistle [4] is also associated with Peter: it is the apostle's discourse in Acts 10 stating that 'God raised up (Jesus) the third day, and shewed him openly, not to all the people, but unto witnesses chosen before of God: even to us, who did eat and drink with him, after he rose from the dead.' It could hardly have been lost on the congregation in St. Peter's that, gathered round the altar in front of the apostle's tomb, they too were eating and drinking with the risen Lord.[5]

The stational church on Tuesday was St. Paul's, so the epistle is taken from Paul's sermon at Antioch of Pisidia in Acts 13: 'And we declare unto you glad tidings, how that the promise which was made unto the fathers, God hath fulfilled the same unto us their children, in that he hath raised up Jesus again.' In the gospel it is told how Jesus appeared to the eleven in Jerusalem and 'opened their understanding, that they might understand the scriptures.'

The Wednesday stational church was St. Lawrence-without-the-Walls. The saint in whose honour the church is dedicated

[4] For convenience I have used the word 'epistle' to describe the first of the two readings at mass, even when the passage is taken from Acts.

[5] Mass was said in front of the tomb until Gregory the Great constructed a pavement in the presbytery of St. Peter's and placed an altar *over* the site between 594 and 604.

72

was one of the most popular of the Roman martyrs, and it is typical of the age that the manner of the saint's death should have influenced the choice of the gospel—the story of the risen Christ preparing a breakfast for the disciples with 'a fire of coals there, and fish laid thereon'! The invitation, 'Come and dine,' was also an invitation to the congregation to share in the sacramental breakfast with the triumphant Lord. The passage is packed with baptismal and eucharistic symbolism—the sea, the ship, the fishes, the meal. The same whimsy that selected the gospel also seems to have guided the choice of the epistle: it is part of Peter's sermon outside the Beautiful Gate of the temple—and St. Lawrence's is on the Via Tiburtina outside the Porta Maggiore of the city of Rome.

On Thursday the baptismal motif is sounded by the epistle, which tells of Philip's encounter with the Ethiopian eunuch. The gospel, John 20: 11–18, is about the appearance to Mary Magdalene and continues the reading of John 20: 1–10, which is set for Saturday. This unchronological arrangement stems from the time when Saturday was the octave day and had John 20: 19–31 as its lection: it completed the *lectio continua* of this chapter of the Fourth Gospel during Easter week. In Gregory's time the verses were distributed 1–10 on Monday, 11–18 on Thursday, and 19–31 on Saturday. Later the Monday gospel was changed to the present passage from Luke 24. Then, when Low Sunday became the octave day and took over the Saturday gospel, the gap was filled by the old Monday lection. (For Anglicans, this complicated game of 'all change' ended when Cranmer put John 20: 1–10 back at the beginning of the week as the gospel for Easter Day.)

The resurrection theme appears in the graduals from Monday to Friday and in the alleluia verses of the Saturday and Low Sunday; it is also the subject of the offertory sentences on Monday, Saturday and Low Sunday. In the communion sentences of Tuesday and Wednesday, however, it is mingled with the baptismal theme, as it is also in the Friday epistle: 'Baptism doth now save us . . . by the resurrection of Jesus Christ, who is gone up into heaven, and is on the right hand of God.'

The baptismal theme knits together some of the introits and their antiphons of the octave, based on texts which are intended to draw out the analogy between the sacrament of initiation and the exodus from Egypt. The introits are taken from psalms which recall the mighty acts of God in thanksgiving and praise: 'O give thanks unto the Lord, and call upon his name: tell the people what things he hath done' (Monday, Tuesday and Saturday); 'O sing unto the Lord a new song: sing unto the Lord, all the whole earth' (Wednesday); 'O sing unto the Lord a new song: for he hath done marvellous things' (Thursday). The introit antiphons of Friday and Saturday and the offertory of Friday also refer to the exodus: 'The Lord hath brought them out safely: and overwhelmed their enemies with the sea. . . . The Lord hath brought forth his people with joy: and his chosen with gladness. . . . This day shall be unto you for a memorial: and ye shall keep it a feast to the Lord throughout your generations: ye shall keep it a feast by an ordinance for ever.'

The entry into a land flowing with milk and honey is remembered in the Monday introit and the Thursday offertory: 'In the day of your solemnity, saith the Lord, I will bring you into a land flowing with milk and honey.' The *Apostolic Tradition* of Hippolytus relates how the neophytes, when they made their first Communion, were given cups to drink, one of milk and honey and the other of water. The custom persisted as long as adults were baptized at Easter or on Whitsunday—an old sacramentary has blessings of milk, honey and water for the purpose. The origins of this little ceremony are a mystery. It may be a realization of biblical symbolism, or it may be the last traces of the agape meal of which the eucharist was once a part.[6]

The waters of baptism are figured in the introit and offertory of Tuesday and in the introit of Friday: 'The water of wisdom hath he given them to drink; and he shall exalt them for ever'; 'the Lord thundered out of heaven: and the Highest gave his thunder: and the springs of water were seen'; 'the Lord hath brought them out safely; and overwhelmed their enemies with the sea.'

Baptism brings Christians into the promised land of the Church. Hence the Thursday communion sentence sings: 'Ye are a peculiar people, show ye forth the praises of him; who hath called you out of darkness into his marvellous light.' The introit consists of the last two verses of the song in Chapter 10 of the Wisdom of Solomon which tells how God's wisdom

[6] E. C. Whitaker, *The Baptismal Liturgy*, p. 51.

74

delivered 'a holy people and a blameless seed from a nation of oppressors' by bringing them out of the Red Sea and leading them 'through much water': 'Thy victorious hand, O Lord, have they magnified, with one accord: for wisdom hath opened the mouth of the dumb, and made eloquent the tongues of them that cannot speak.' And since the sacrament brings Christians through the judgment which God has passed on the prince of this world, the Church is able to echo our Lord's words as they assemble for the eucharist: 'Come, ye blessed of my Father, inherit the kingdom: which hath been prepared for you from the foundation of the world' (introit antiphon, Wednesday).

The baptismal theme is caught up in the Thursday epistle, the story of Philip and the Ethiopian eunuch, and the Friday gospel, the Dominical commission: 'Go ye, therefore, and teach all nations, baptizing them in the name of the Father, and of the Son, and of the Holy Ghost: teaching them to observe all things whatsoever I have commanded you.' The commission is repeated in the communion sentence of that day, and in the introit the people are summoned to listen to Christ's teaching: 'Hear my law, O my people: Incline your ears unto the words of my mouth.' 'As new-born babes,' the introit antiphon intones to the neophytes on Low Sunday, 'desire ye the guileless milk of the word,' and then raises its voice in joy: 'Sing we merrily unto God our helper: make a cheerful noise unto the God of Jacob.'

Psalm 78, a song about the exodus, provides the offertory for Wednesday; it is eucharistic in character and responds to the gospel account on that day of Christ breakfasting with his disciples on the sea shore: 'The Lord opened the doors of heaven: and rained down manna upon them for to eat: he gave them food from heaven: so man did eat angels' food.'

On the octave day, the neophytes took off their baptismal garments at the beginning of mass. The Saturday epistle, selected when this was the octave day, still echoes the ancient custom, for it reminds the newly-baptised of the more important things which they have discarded: 'Laying aside therefore all malice, and all guile, and hypocrisies, and envies, and all evil speakings, as new-born babes desire the sincere milk of the word: that ye may grow thereby: if so be ye have tasted that the Lord is gracious. To whom coming, as unto a living stone, disallowed indeed of men, but chosen of God,

75

and precious: ye also, as lively stones, are built up a spiritual house, an holy priesthood, to offer up spiritual sacrifices, acceptable to God by Jesus Christ.' They have put on instead another garment, says the communion sentence: 'As many of you as have been baptized into Christ have put on Christ, alleluia.' And then the alleluia and its verse give the newly-baptized the text for expressing their thankful reply: 'Alleluia, alleluia. This is the day which the Lord hath made: we will rejoice and be glad in it. Praise the Lord, ye servants, O praise the name of the Lord.' In the offertory there is a flourish of good wishes all round: 'Blessed is he that cometh in the name of the Lord: we have wished you good luck, ye that are of the house of the Lord: God is the Lord who hath shewed us light.'

The epistle of Low Sunday sums up all that the congregations have learnt in the liturgy of the previous fifteen days: 'Whatsoever is born of God overcometh the world: and this is the victory that overcometh the world, even our faith. Who is he that overcometh the world, but he that believeth that Jesus is the Son of God? This is he that came by water and blood. And it is the Spirit that beareth witness, because the Spirit is truth. For there are three that bear record in heaven: the Father, the Word, and the Holy Ghost: and these three are one. And there are three that bear witness in earth: the spirit, and the water, and the blood: and these three agree in one. If we receive the witness of men, the witness of God is greater: for this is the witness of God which he hath testified of his Son. He that believeth on the Son of God hath the witness in himself.' The alleluia verse is a reminder, taken from the gospel, that this is the octave day: 'After eight days. . . .' The communion urges the faithful to approach the altar and to accept in the sacrament the tangible evidence of the resurrection that Thomas was offered: 'Reach hither thy hand, and behold the print of the nails, alleluia: and be not faithless, but believing.'[7] So the octave closes with the intention expressed in the words of the Low Sunday collect: 'Grant, we beseech thee, Almighty God, that we who have celebrated the paschal rites may, through thy bounty, ever cleave to them in our life and conversation. . . .'

[7] For a more detailed analysis of the lections and chants in the Roman missal see the contributions by A. Chavasse in *L'Eglise en prière,* ed. A. G. Martimort, pp. 713ff. and 758ff., and 'Le Dimanche et le temps de Paques' by P. Jounel in *La Maison-Dieu,* No. 67 (1961), pp. 163ff.

VIII. *From 'Good Shepherd' Sunday to Whitsun*

With the establishment of Ascension Day and Whitsunday, the Sundays within the great Fifty Days took on something of the expectancy we can detect in the Lucan narrative between the resurrection, the ascension, and the coming of the Holy Spirit. This atmosphere permeates the gospels and some of the chants. The epistles for these Sundays are not affected by it, for they were borrowed from a series of lections in the Catholic Epistles that were originally read in the weeks between January and the beginning of Lent. They are not particularly paschal in character; if they serve any purpose at all, it is to exhort the faithful and the newly-baptized to remain steadfast in their Christian profession.

The gospels, on the other hand, are part of the *lectio continua* of St. John, which begins in the Roman missal with chapter 1 on Christmas Day and continues down to chapter 13 on Maundy Thursday, chapters 18 and 19 on Good Friday, and chapters 20 and 21 in Easter week. Chapters 14 to 17 are used on the Sundays after Easter. The fact that these chapters are out of order chronologically did not worry the compilers. The whole of St. John is post-paschal in its outlook, and these selections from the discourses of Christ fit in appropriately with the expectant atmosphere of the period.

This scheme was spoilt, however, by a change in the gospel reading for Easter II. At one time the congregation heard St. John 14: 1–13, 'I go to prepare a place for you.' When the epistles were borrowed from the older list, the first reading of this day became 1 Peter 2: 21–5, ending with the words, 'For ye were as sheep going astray: but are now returned unto the shepherd and bishop of your souls.' The idea of Jesus as the good shepherd was extremely popular in Christian piety, as early paintings and mosaics indicate, and the reference to 'shepherd' in the epistle led to the substitution of the old gospel reading for another one that harmonized with the theme: 'I am the good shepherd' (John 10: 11–16). The words of Jesus in this passage also became the communion chant.

The gospel for Easter III announces the departure and the second coming of Christ: 'Ye now therefore have sorrow, but I will see you again, and your heart shall rejoice: and your joy no man taketh from you.' The communion chant repeats the promise: 'A little while, and ye shall not see me; and again, a little while and ye shall see me, because I go to the Father.' In spite of the alleluias, the mood is more sober than previously; but the paschal joy returns in the introit psalm: 'Rejoice in the Lord, O ye righteous: for it becometh well the just to be thankful,' and again in the offertory: 'O be joyful in God, all ye lands; sing ye praises unto the honour of his name: make his praise to be exceeding glorious. Say unto God, O how wonderful art thou in thy works, O Lord! through the greatness of thy power shall thine enemies be found liars unto thee.' These verses are taken from Psalm 66, which also provides the offertory chants for Easter IV and Easter V and the introit for Easter V. The repeated use of this psalm helps to retain in the liturgy the spirit of the *laetissimum spatium* during the Sundays of Eastertide.

Other chants have the same effect: 'Praise the Lord, O my soul: while I live will I praise the Lord: yea, as long as I have any being, I will sing praises unto my God' (offertory, Easter III); 'O sing unto the Lord a new song: for the Lord hath done marvellous things: in the sight of the nations hath he showed his righteousness. With his right hand, and with his holy arm: hath he gotten himself the victory' (introit, Easter IV); 'With the voice of singing declare ye this, and let it be heard: utter it even unto the end of the earth: the Lord hath delivered his people. O be joyful in God, all ye lands, sing praises unto the honour of his name: make his praise to be glorious. . . . O sing unto the Lord: sing unto the Lord, and praise his name: be telling of his salvation from day to day' (introit and communion, Easter V).

The gospel for Easter IV explains that the departure of Jesus is necessary because it is a condition of sending the Holy Spirit. 'I tell you the truth: it is expedient for you that I go away: for if I go not away, the Comforter will not come unto you: but if I depart, I will send him unto you.' This gospel, together with that of the following Sunday, turns the thoughts of the faithful towards the end of Eastertide and the eschatological harvest in which the week of weeks finds its culmination: 'And when he is come, he will reprove the world of sin, and of righteousness, and of judgement.' This fore-knowledge of the coming judgment explains the use of Psalm 98 as an introit: 'In the sight of the nations he hath showed his righteousness.'

On Easter V the gospel assures the congregation of their acceptance by God: 'At that day ye shall ask in my name: and I say not unto you, that I will pray the Father for you: for the Father himself loveth you, because ye have loved me, and have believed that I came out from God. I came forth from the Father, and am come into the world: again, I leave the world, and go to the Father.' And the congregation reply in the offertory: 'O praise the Lord our God, ye people, and make the voice of his praise to be heard who holdeth our soul in life, and suffereth not our feet to slip: praised be the Lord who hath not cast out my prayer, nor turned his mercy from me, alleluia.' Although the departure is about to take place, the faithful can still 'be telling of his salvation from day to day' (communion sentence) for the Lord goes only to intercede for them before the Father and to unite them for ever with God in the fellowship of the Holy Spirit.

The oscillation between expectancy and assurance continues in the introit of the Sunday after Ascension Day: 'Hearken unto my voice, O Lord, when I cry unto thee: unto thee my heart hath said, Thy face have I sought, thy face, Lord, will I seek: O hide not thy face from me. The Lord is my light, and my salvation: whom then shall I fear?' The epistle urges watchfulness: 'The end of all things is at hand,' and the alleluia chant carols the ascended Lord, 'Alleluia, alleluia. The Lord reigneth over all the heathen: God sitteth upon his holy seat.'

The faithful are reminded of the Lord's promise in the gospel as they look forward to Whitsunday: 'When the Comforter is come, whom I will send unto you from the Father, even the Spirit of truth, which proceedeth from the Father, he shall testify of me, and ye shall also bear witness, because ye have been with me from the beginning.' The Church is to be equipped for her mission to the world, and as her members receive communion on this Sunday before Whitsunday they hear a verse from John 17, the prayer of Christ their high

79

priest: 'Father, while I was with them, I kept those that thou gavest me: and now I come to thee: I pray not that thou shouldest take them out of the world: but that thou shouldest keep them from the evil.'

The mass of the Sunday after the Ascension was celebrated by the Pope in the Pantheon of Agrippa. Early in the seventh century Boniface IV had converted this massive structure into a Christian church and hallowed it by burying within its walls the relics of many Roman martyrs. The gospel for the day is the Lord's warning about persecution: 'They shall put you out of the synagogues: yea, the time cometh, that whosoever killeth you will think that he doeth God service.' It must have echoed poignantly round the circling walls of St. Mary of the Martyrs, as the Pantheon is called.

When Ascension Day and Whitsunday acquired the rank of feasts, they were both given vigils. All that remains of the vigil of the Ascension is a gospel and an epistle—the former being the high priestly prayer of John 17 ('I come to thee'), the latter a passage from the Ephesian letter with its comments on the 'ascension psalm' ('Now that he ascended, what is it but that he also descended first unto the lower parts of the earth?'). The chants are taken from the preceding Sunday. The Whitsunday vigil was modelled on the vigil of Holy Saturday.

Ascension Day has the first verses of Acts 1 as an epistle and the Lucan account of the Ascension as a gospel. The introit antiphon is also from Acts 1: 'Ye men of Galilee, why marvel ye gazing up into heaven? In like manner as ye have seen him going up into heaven, so shall he come again.' The remainder of the chants are taken from the 'ascension psalms' 47 and 68 with which we are familiar: 'O clap your hands together, all ye people: O sing unto God with the voice of melody' (introit); 'God is gone up with a merry noise, and the Lord with the sound of the trumpet. Alleluia. The Lord in the holy place of Sinai, ascending up on high, hath led captivity captive. Alleluia' (alleluia verses and offertory); 'Sing ye to the Lord, who ascended above the heaven of heavens, to the sunrising' (communion).

The theology of the Ascension is expressed in the proper preface: 'Through Christ our Lord, who after his resurrection manifestly appeared to all his disciples, and in their sight ascended up into heaven, that he might make us partakers of his Godhead,' and in the *infra actionem:* 'Joining in communion, and celebrating the most sacred day whereon our Lord, thine only-begotten Son, set at the right hand of thy glory the substance of our frailty united with himself.'

The lections and chants of Whitsunday are those of a festival of the Holy Spirit, not those of a closing assembly of the great Fifty Days. The epistle is the account of the descent of the Holy Spirit in Acts 2, and the communion chant repeats the central verse ('Suddenly there came a sound from heaven as of a rushing mighty wind, where they were sitting: and they were all filled with the Holy Ghost, speaking the wonderful works of God'). The gospel spells out the book of the new covenant: 'If ye love me, keep my commandments. . . . The Comforter, which is the Holy Ghost, whom the Father will send in my name, he shall teach you all things, and bring all things to your remembrance, whatsoever I have said unto you.' On this day the Church knows 'I am in the Father, and ye in me, and I in you.'

The preface praises God that Christ, 'ascending above all heavens and sitting at thy right hand, poured forth this day the promised Holy Spirit upon the sons of adoption. Wherefore with exceeding joy the whole round world exulteth. . . .' Even the *infra actionem*, normally the more restrained part of the canon, acknowledges the 'most sacred day of Pentecost whereon the Holy Ghost appeared in tongues innumerable.'

The chants resound with joy at the gift. 'The Spirit of the Lord hath filled the whole world; and that which containeth all things hath knowledge of the voice, alleluia, alleluia, alleluia. Let God arise, and let his enemies be scattered: let them also that hate him flee before him' (introit); 'O send forth thy Spirit and they shall be made, and thou shalt renew the face of the earth. Alleluia. Come, Holy Ghost, fill the hearts of thy faithful: and kindle in them the fire of thy love' (alleluia verse). The offertory antiphon ('Stablish the thing, O God, that thou hast wrought in us') was introduced into the rite of confirmation about the tenth century.

If the Whitsunday liturgy looks back at all, it is not to Easter but to Ascension Day. The theological interdependence of the ascension of Christ and the descent of the Spirit is demonstrated in the proper preface, which we have quoted, and in the use of Psalm 68 in the chants of both days. In the *Hanc igitur* is there a link with Easter Day—this portion of

81

the canon is set for Easter Day and Whitsunday and their respective octaves—but only because Whitsunday, like Easter, was a baptism day: 'This oblation therefore of our bounden service, as also of all thy family, which we offer unto thee on behalf of these also, whom thou hast vouchsafed to regenerate by water and the Holy Ghost, granting them remission of all their sins. . . .'

The reading of Acts during Easter week has influenced the choice of the epistles for the Whitsun octave.[1] Like their prototypes, they are also baptismal in character, but adjustments are made to stress the work of the Holy Spirit. For example, the lection for the Monday of both the Easter and the Whitsun octaves comes from the same chapter in Acts (10), but whereas the Easter Monday reading ends with the last words of Peter's sermon ('To him give all the prophets witness, that through his name whosoever believeth in him shall receive remission of sins'), the Whit Monday reading goes on to tell of the Gentile Pentecost ('While Peter yet spake these words, the Holy Ghost fell on all of them which heard the word . . .').

Tuesday once had the reading Acts 13: 44–52, but this was moved to Saturday, probably because of its reference to the sabbath ('The next sabbath day came almost the whole city together to hear the word of God. . . . And the disciples were filled with joy, and with the Holy Ghost'). It was lost when the Embertide lections were reintroduced into the Whitsun octave. Tuesday now has the account of the 'confirmation' in Samaria, Acts 8: 14–17. The epistles of Ember Wednesday, Acts 5: 12–16, and Thursday, Acts 8: 5–8, demonstrate the spiritual triumph of Pentecost with the expulsion of evil spirits by the apostles. The first of the three lections on Ember Wednesday is Peter's comment on the Joel prophecy in his sermon on the day of Pentecost, Acts 2: 14–21. The Friday epistle was once Acts 21: 22–8, but it was replaced by an Embertide lection, Joel 2: 22–7 ('The floors shall be full of wheat, and the fats shall overflow with wine and oil').

This Joel reading is continued as the first lection on the Saturday to become thoroughly pentecostal with its promise to 'pour out my Spirit upon all flesh.' The fifth reading, from the Song of the Three Young Men ('The fire touched them

[1] The octaves of Easter and Whitsun were retained in the recent revision, but the vigil of Pentecost was abolished.

not, neither hurt nor troubled them'), was also in keeping with the octave, but the remaining three—harvesting regulations from Deuteronomy and Leviticus—belong to the Embertide. As it happens, they are in the spirit of the season as a harvest time, though they belong to Passover-Unleavened Bread rather than the feast of Weeks. When Romans 8: 18–23 was one of the lections it formed an admirable bridge between the implications of the Jewish and the Christian Pentecost ('ourselves also, which have the firstfruits of the Spirit . . .').

The Embertide gospels for Friday, Luke 5: 17–26 (the healing of the paralytic) and for Saturday, Luke 4: 38–44 (the healing of Simon's mother-in-law) have been retained, but the Embertide gospel for Wednesday has been replaced by John 6: 44–52, the 'Bread of life' discourse which contains the pentecostal theme of a spiritual and a sacramental harvest. Thursday's gospel, Luke 9: 1–6, is the account of Christ giving his disciples power over evil spirits and, like the epistle for that day, demonstrates the consequence of his victory in the spiritual realm.

This leaves us to account for the gospels of Monday, John 3: 16–21 ('God so loved the world') and Tuesday, John 10: 1–10 ('I am the door of the sheep'). The first of these continues the reading from the following Sunday (Trinity Sunday, the opening of the discourse with Nicodemus) and the second consists of the earlier verses of John 10 which were not read on Easter II. It may well be that they were selected for this reason, but Fr. Jungmann has another suggestion. He points out that the Monday and Tuesday after the great Fifty Days were the time when public penance was resumed after the suspension of the discipline during Eastertide. Penances were normally imposed at the beginning of Lent, and like the first Monday and Tuesday in Lent, these gospels are concerned with Judgment and the door of the sheepfold. The stations for these masses are the same as those for the first two days in Lent, St. Peter ad Vincula and St. Anastasis, churches in Rome which were particularly associated with the supervision of those undergoing penance.[2]

Many of the chants in the Whitsun octave are borrowed from Easter week—the offertories of Monday, Tuesday and Friday, and the introit psalms of Monday and Tuesday. The antiphons of these introits are taken from paschal-baptismal

[2] J. A. Jungmann, *Pastoral Liturgy*, pp. 238ff.

texts. Other chants were chosen from appropriate passages of scripture. The communion chants of Monday, Tuesday and Wednesday were all taken from a gospel that was once read on Whitsunday, John 14: 15–31 (now the gospel of the vigil). The Wednesday introit and its antiphon are verses from the 'pentecostal' Psalm 68, and so is the communion chant for that day. Thursday, which remained vacant until the end of the seventh century, has been filled with the chants of Whitsunday itself. As the last day of the octave, Saturday has a particularly appropriate text from Romans 8 as its introit antiphon, taken from a lection which was at one time read on that day but which is now the epistle for Trinity IV: 'The love of God is shed abroad in our hearts: by the Holy Spirit which dwelleth in us.'

IX. *The Great Fifty Days in the Prayer Book*

In composing a simplified liturgy in the vernacular the English reformers swept away much of the material we have been examining in the last two chapters. The 1549 and the 1552 Prayer Books mark stages in the process. It is not necessary for us to follow this process in detail throughout the great Fifty Days, so we will only take as an example the changes made on Easter Day itself.

The 1549 proper for Easter Day began with the formularies from the Sarum missal used for the procession from the 'sepulchre' on Easter morning—a verse and antiphon with alleluias, a versicle and response, and a collect. These were to be used before mattins. Then, after listing the psalms and the lessons for the office, the Prayer Book provided two separate Communion Services, each with an introit psalm, a collect, an epistle and a gospel.

The introits were Psalms 16 and 3 respectively. Although some of their verses could be used as a meditation on the resurrection ('Thou shalt not leave my soul in hell: neither shalt thou suffer thy holy one to see corruption . . . I laid me down and slept: and rose up again, for the Lord sustained me') they are not among the chants traditionally used at the eucharist on Easter Day.

The epistle for the first Communion Service and the two lections for the second were taken from the masses of the Easter vigil and of Easter Day in the missal. A few additional verses were added, but these did not make much difference except in the case of the epistle in the first service.

The lection in the Roman rite is Colossians 3: 1–4, 'If ye then be risen with Christ, seek those things which are above, where Christ sitteth on the right hand of God. Set your affection on things above, not on things on the earth. For ye are dead, and your life is hid with Christ in God. When Christ, who is our life, shall appear, then shall ye also appear with him in glory.'

As a short compact reading this was admirable for the day

of resurrection and the first of the great Fifty Days. It lifted the thoughts of the Church to the risen and reigning Lord and to their ultimate unity with him—a unity prefigured during the most joyful season itself. But the English reformers evidently wanted to remind their fellow churchmen of the implications of Easter in terms of moral conduct, for they added verses 5, 6 and 7: 'Mortify, therefore, your members which are upon the earth; fornication, uncleanness, inordinate affection, evil concupiscence, and covetousness, which is idolatry: for which things' sake the wrath of God cometh on the children of disobedience: in the which ye also walked some time, when ye lived in them.'

The effect of the added verses was to give the lection a rather sombre character more suitable for Lent than Eastertide.

The gospel for the mass of the Easter vigil had been Matthew 28: 1–7, the earthquake, the rolling back of the stone, and the angel's message to the women—a dramatic pericope with apocalyptic overtones. The reformers dropped this and instead substituted John 20: 1–10, the gospel of the mass on Saturday of the octave. (Anglicans still hear this unsatisfactory epistle and this excellent gospel when they go to church to receive communion on Easter morning.)

The collect for the first service was that of the Easter morning mass ('Almighty God, who through thine only begotten Son Jesus Christ hast overcome death, and opened unto us the gate of everlasting life . . .'). For the second service a new collect was written ('Almighty Father, who hast given thine only Son to die for our sins, and to rise again for our justification . . .'). This collect was also set for Low Sunday.

The 1552 revision laid down that the anthems were to take the place of the *Venite* at mattins, but the alleluias, the versicle and response, and the collect belonging to the 'sepulchre' procession were scrapped. The introit psalms were abolished (as they were for all the propers throughout the year) and the second Easter Communion Service was dropped (though its collect remains that for Low Sunday).

Finally, in 1661 a new anthem (1 Corinthians 15: 20–2) was added to those at the beginning of the proper.

Revisions for the rest of the great Fifty Days followed much the same pattern. The Sundays in Eastertide, Ascension

Day and Whitsunday kept the epistles and gospels from the masses for those days in the Roman missal; the lections for the Mondays and Tuesdays in Easter week and Whit week were for the octave masses.

But there were modifications. The epistle for Easter II was lengthened and that for Easter III was shortened—in the latter case to give the reading from 1 Peter 2 an ending well known to every communicant in the Anglican Church: 'Honour all men. Love the brotherhood. Fear God. Honour the king.'

The gospels for Low Sunday and Whitsunday were also shortened, and one verse was added to the lection for Easter IV and three verses to that of Easter V. (Details of these variations are shown in the tables printed in Appendix A, p. 100.)

Limiting the number of the readings at the Holy Communion Service to two meant the loss of the Old Testament passages connected with the great Fifty Days. Lections from the Old Testament were provided, of course, for mattins and evensong, and it was undoubtedly the reformers' intention that these offices should contribute the main diet in the ministry of the Word; but even so it was not until 1661 that an attempt was made to give evensong on Easter Day and mattins and evensong on Ascension Day and Whitsunday appropriate Old Testament lessons.

The proper prefaces for Easter Day and Ascension Day and their octaves were taken from the Roman rite; that for Whitsunday and the following week was a new composition. The Rogations and Ember Days remain in the calendar, but are not given any special lections—they have a 'black letter' status. Two collects for Embertide and some prayers of a rogationary nature were printed elsewhere in the Prayer Book.

Following the 1928 Prayer Book, the *Alternative Services First Series* (1966) restore some of the services rejected by the reformers. Epistles and gospels are provided for the remaining days of the Easter and Whitsun octaves, based largely on the masses for those days in the Roman missal. Epistles and gospels are also set for the Rogation Days: Monday's lections are new (James 5: 7–11 and Luke 6: 36–42), Tuesday's are from the *Litaniae minores,* and Wednesday's are those of the vigil. Easter Day has an extra collect. The proper prefaces for

Easter Day and Ascension Day are the same as those in the Prayer Book, though the former is to be used throughout the forty days until the eve of the Ascension. With the Whitsun preface, however, an alternative is provided which, closely following the opening of the Roman proper preface, launches out into a reference to the missionary work of the Church in the power of the Holy Spirit:

Roman	*1966 (1928)*
Who going up above all the heavens, and sitting at thy right hand (on this day) sent forth the Holy Spirit, as he promised, on the children of adoption. Wherefore does the whole world rejoice with exceeding great joy over all the earth; and the hosts above and the angelic powers also join in singing the hymn of thy glory, saying without ceasing, Holy, holy, holy. . . .	Who after that he had ascended up far above all the heavens, and was sat down at the right hand of thy Majesty: Did as at this time pour forth upon the Universal Church thy Holy and Life-giving Spirit: That through his glorious power the joy of the everlasting gospel might go forth into all the world: Whereby we have been brought out of darkness and error into the clear light and true knowledge of thee, and of thy Son our Saviour Jesus Christ. Therefore with Angels, &c. . . . [1]

The *Alternative Services First Series* publish, in an appendix to the Holy Communion Service, Old Testament lessons which can be used in addition to the epistle and gospel on Sundays and on Holy Days. They are taken from the *Book of Common Prayer according to the use of the Church of India, Pakistan, Burma, and Ceylon* (1960) and we find some familiar pericopes in the list chosen for the great Fifty Days:

[1] In the *Draft Order for Holy Communion* in the *Second Series* the following is set from Ascension Day to the Saturday after Pentecost: 'For by the gift of that same Spirit thou hast empowered thy people to preach the Gospel among the nations, and to serve thee acceptably as a royal priesthood.'

Easter Day: Exodus 12: 21-8
The regulations for the sacrifice of the Lord's passover.

Low Sunday: Ezekiel 37: 1-10
The prophecy of the valley of dry bones.

Easter II: Ezekiel 34: 11-16c
The Lord God as the shepherd.

Easter III: Genesis 45: 3-10
Joseph makes himself known to his brothers.

Easter IV: Job 19: 21-7b
'I know that my Redeemer liveth.'

Easter V: Joel 2: 21-6
The former and the latter rain (an old Embertide lection).

Ascension Day: Daniel 7: 13-14
The Ancient of Days.

Ascension I: 2 Kings 2: 9-15
The ascension of Elijah.

Whitsunday: Deuteronomy 16: 9-12
The commandment to observe the feast of Weeks.[2]

There is not very much we can add by way of comment to this development. The treatment of the great Fifty Days is still starkly historical as it is in the Roman missal, leading the worshipper from Easter Day to Ascension Day with the disciples and then on to the expectation of the Holy Spirit's advent on Whitsunday. The absence of the chants means that something of the joyful nature of the season has been lost, for it is these verses that keep the character of the *laetissimum spatium* alive in the missal. But the Anglican Church has made up for this in the last hundred years by introducing hymns into the Communion Service. Where hymn-writers have drawn on traditional scriptural material for Easter Day,

[2] *Alternative Services, First Series* (1966), p. 65. Some Prayer Books in the Anglican Communion have added a second epistle and gospel for Easter Day, e.g. Hebrews 13:20-1 and Mark 16:1-8.

Ascension Day and Whitsunday, they have restored to the ministry of the Word in the great Fify Days much that was formerly provided in introits, graduals, offertories and communion chants.

J. M. Neale and other compilers have translated medieval hymns containing paschal imagery:

> *The Lamb's high banquet called to share,*
> *Arrayed in garments white and fair,*
> *The Red Sea past, we fain would sing*
> *To Jesus our triumphant King.*[3]

—though it is a pity the verse does not suggest that the garments could also be those of baptismal innocence. The neglect of the traditional paschaltide cry of praise in the Prayer Book liturgy is made good by its appearance in many hymns for the season; Bishop Christopher Wordsworth began his great Easter hymn with it and in other verses re-echoes the harvest theme of the feast of Weeks:

> *Alleluia! Alleluia!*
> *Hearts to heaven and voices raise . . .*
> *Christ is risen, Christ the firstfruits*
> *Of the holy harvest field . . .*
> *Christ is risen, we are risen;*
> *Shed upon us heavenly grace.*[4]

In one of Wordsworth's Ascensiontide hymns we hear again the angels' question of the ascending Christ at the gates of heaven:

> *Who is this that comes in glory,*
> *With the trump of jubilee?* [5]

And John Keble linked the Jewish and the Christian meaning of the feast of Pentecost in some famous lines:

[3] *English Hymnal*, 125; *Ancient and Modern Revised*, 129.
[4] *E.H.*, 127; *A. & M.R.*, 137.
[5] *E.H.*, 145; *A. & M.R.*, 148.

When God of old came down from heaven,
In power and wrath he came;
Before his feet the clouds were riven,
Half darkness and half flame.

But when he came a second time,
He came in power and love;
Softer than gale at morning prime
Hovered his holy Dove.[6]

The purpose of a hymn in the eucharistic liturgy, like that of a chant, is to put into the mouth of the congregation words through which they can express their response to the ministry of the Word (and to the ministry of the Sacrament). To do this, they do not necessarily have to re-tell in verse form the passage they have just listened to—like those tedious Easter hymns which narrate every detail through innumerable lines. Consequently any suitable hymn of praise and thanksgiving can be used for the great Fifty Days, even if they are not set by the editors under the Eastertide or Whitsunday sections of the hymn book.

[6] *E.H.*, 156; *A. & M.R.*, 154.

X. *The Crown of the Year*

When the peace of Constantine confronted the Church with her great opportunity for mission throughout the whole of society, the elaboration of the calendar was one of the many changes that were made in her attempt to fulfil that task. The liturgical year developed because the Church was involved in the world more than she had ever been since the first Pentecost. The pilgrimage processions and stations in Jerusalem, the ceremonies of Holy Week and Easter Week in Rome, the Rogations of farmers and serfs in southern Gaul—all these originated because ordinary people looked to the Church for comfort and hope, and the Church found it valuable to give that comfort and proclaim that hope aided by such observances.

To-day, the Church's opportunity for mission is no less great, but the society and the circumstances within which it is to be fulfilled have changed beyond recognition.

The social customs which have collected round the Christian festivals have smothered their evangelical impact. The commercialization of Christmas has been increasing for years with the growth of leisure and affluence. The popularity of short holidays are having a similar effect on the feasts of Easter and Whitsun, while the significance of Ascension Day has been so completely obscured that in 1925 the Roman Catholic Church instituted another festival, fixed for a Sunday, to celebrate the reign of the ascended Lord in heaven, the feast of Christ the King.

It is practically impossible to use, as a means of mission, the old observances in honour of the truths of the Gospel. Inspired attempts are made at Christmas and Easter to convey the meaning of the incarnation and the resurrection to our post-Christian society through music and drama on the various media of mass communication; but the festivals themselves are on occasions for such presentations, not essential to them.

It is not that the faithful no longer keep the feasts. On the contrary, the congregations observe them with enthusiasm, as the numbers of communicants witness. But they now observe them in a different kind of way. It is not unusual for a communicant to keep Lent and Holy Week in his own parish and then to be miles away on Easter Day. Many clergy find that on Whitsunday their own parishioners have joined in the holiday exodus and that a high proportion of the people in church on that day are visitors.*

We must also take into account the fact that an increasing amount of the Church's pastoral work is undertaken in social groupings which are more affected by national holidays than the residents in a parish. The eucharistic assemblies of the guild churches and of various chaplaincies—in industry, in the services, and in schools, colleges and universities—are non-existent during the greater festivals.

In the end, it may not matter if the members of the Church keep these feasts away from their usual congregations. Yet something precious in the rhythm of the Church's year is lost by those who normally worship together, if they disperse just at the moment when they would celebrate the mighty acts of God. There is an interruption in the proclamation of the Word of God through the liturgy to that group, and an interruption in their response to it, which is more unsatisfactory than if they scattered, say, for two or three Sundays in Trinitytide.

Another factor that we must take into consideration—and one that is difficult both to describe and to assess—is the contemporary theological climate. We have also seen during this short survey that the teaching of the Church had a penetrating influence on the form and content of the liturgical year and that the development of doctrine was shadowed by changes in the calendar.

Now we are in the midst of a widespread re-examination of the Church's teaching which is sharpening the division between the *lex orandi* of the liturgical year and the *lex credendi* of Christian thought.

It is not that Christians are ceasing to believe in the historical reality behind the incarnation and the resurrection and

* Though this situation might be modified if some of the public holidays are moved away from the religious festivals.

93

the gift of the Holy Spirit (except on the fringes of Christian commitment). It is that the results of biblical criticism over the last century or so have shifted the Church's outlook away from the reasons why the fortieth of the great Fifty Days, for example, was chosen to commemorate the ascension.

To put the matter very shortly, we now recognize that, in the New Testament, stories with a profound symbolic significance are told in a matter-of-fact way that has misled the literalistic Western mind. When we read that the risen Christ was 'taken up' into heaven and that a cloud received him out of the disciples' sight, we are certain that Luke was not thinking about the cosmological implications of the narrative. Heaven was no more a *place* for him than it was to any other biblical writer.

With the marriage of Hebrew thought and Greek science in the apostolic age, a literalness of interpretation affected the Church's treatment of scripture which can be seen, at an early stage, in the adoption of the fortieth day as a festival of the ascension event and, at a later stage, by the cruder representations of heaven and the ascension in medieval art. We would not have to demythologize the Lucan text if earlier generations of Christians had not accepted it as a piece of descriptive cosmology.

The instructed churchman can take these difficulties in his stride and rejoice in a beautiful festival of Christ's kingship and glory, but they become much more serious when we think of the calendar in terms of the Church's mission. We might ask ourselves if we are laying the foundations of faith or of incredulity when we withdraw children from school on the morning of Ascension Day to hear Acts 1: 1–11 read as the epistle and then to join in singing 'Hail, the day that sees him rise!' [1]

But there is another movement of thought within the Church which is powerfully influencing her life in our age and which has to be taken into consideration. This is the growing realization of what it means to belong to the Church as a fellowship of the Holy Spirit. The prayers and discussions for Christian unity and the acceptance by the laity of a fuller

[1] There is much to be said for using the lections for the vigil of the Ascension (Ephesians 4:7–13 and John 17:1–11a) or those for the feast of Christ the King instead (Colossians 1:12–20 and John 18:33–7).

ministry within the Church's mission have resulted in an awareness of the charismatic nature of the Christian community. At a popular level this movement has manifested itself in individuals or groups of churchmen seeking to employ the gifts of the Spirit for the building up and functioning of the Body of Christ; at an academic level its most striking manifestation is the dogmatic constitution *De ecclesia* of Vatican II with its insistence that 'it is not only through the sacraments and Church ministries that the Holy Spirit sanctifies and leads the people of God and enriches it with virtues. Allotting his gifts "to every one according as he will," he distributes special graces among the faithful of every rank.' [2] Churchmen of every tradition are seeing again that Pentecost as well as Passover has its profound significance for each and every baptized person.

We are learning, as we kneel at the foot of the cross, to look beyond Calvary to a faith that rejoices in its liberation from sin rather than to one that is restricted by a sense of utter unworthiness. Perhaps our emphasis on Lent and Good Friday and Easter Day indicates our preoccupation with the need for salvation rather than our knowledge that salvation is something we have been most graciously granted here-and-now. We have to learn once more that, if sin exists and is important, grace is more exceeding abundant.

When we turn to the liturgy of Eastern Christendom we find there a different spirit:

> *Christ is risen and hell is overthrown!*
> *Christ is risen and the demons are fallen!*
> *Christ is risen and life reigns!*

Here is the Church's full Gospel! The words of John Chrysostom, incorporated into the paschal vigil of the Orthodox Churches, sound the tocsin of Christian faith and joy. Here *is* salvation! Here *is* the grace of our Lord Jesus Christ, and the love of God, and the fellowship of the Holy Ghost! [3]

When we reflect on these social and doctrinal developments

[2] *c.* 12.

[3] The 'Pentecostary,' a special service book for Eastertide in the Byzantine liturgy, provides the following rubric on the eve of Easter: 'If one of our brethren returns to the Lord during this holy week of renewal, we sing for him, not the office of the dead, but the office of Easter.'

both within and outside the Church and then consider how they can be fittingly expressed in her worship and in her calendar, there seems a good case for recovering the unity of the great Fifty Days and the spirit of joy and freedom associated with them. We should not exhume the old Pentecost: that would be mere archaeology. Rather we should arrange for an observance of the eight Sundays and the intervening weekdays that sets them above the rest of the liturgical year. They would constitute a festal season celebrating the totality of God's saving act in Christ and through the Holy Spirit, when Christians would be drawn to worship the glory and the majesty of God in a feast of the Church united with her Head. As Lent has now become a period when congregations corporately revert to their pre-baptismal status of catechumens to learn afresh what it means to be a Christian, so the great Fifty Days would become the crown of the Church's year, when her members rejoiced in the risen and reigning Lord and when, united with him in the power of the Holy Spirit, they launched out to participate in his mission in the world.

The most joyful season could become the popular occasion for baptisms, confirmations and first communions; for evangelistic enterprises of different kinds; for a drawing together of separated Christians in ecumenical schemes, especially in a joint ministry to people in a locality. (The ten days between Ascension Day and Whitsunday have been put forward as an alternative to the winter-bound octave of prayer for Christian unity.)

In the eucharist provision could be made for an expression of joy in salvation and of faith in mission. We have noticed some examples in the Roman missal for variations within the eucharistic prayer itself.[4] Would it be possible to limit the use of the *Gloria* to this season and to one or two other feast days? Could we suspend the use of general confessions at services during the great Fifty Days, using instead a general thanksgiving for our redemption and salvation?

But the burden of the task of conveying the spirit of Pentecost would fall on the ministry of the Word. The Church of

[4] The extended use of the proper preface throughout Eastertide in the 1928–66 Anglican revisions is a small step in the right direction. See above, p. 88 n. 1.

England has had some experience of drawing up new lectionaries for mattins and evensong. The 1922–61 series extended the use of suitable readings: the Old Testament pericopes associated with Easter, Ascension Day and Whitsunday have been restored, and Acts is once more read as a *lectio continua* from Low Sunday onwards. Here, at any rate, is something to begin with. What we need is a series of lections for the Sunday eucharists and another series for the weekdays of Eastertide which would do for the Holy Communion Service what the 1922–61 tables do for the offices.

We must revise the calendar with the same methods and objectives with which we are learning to build new churches. It is generally recognized that when a new church is designed it is an error just to copy an older plan. In the flurry of new constructions since the war, critics have compelled architects, advisory committees, clergy and congregations to consider at some depth what they wanted to provide as a place of worship. Before any specifications are listed or plans drawn, they ask what appear to be simple questions, like 'What is a church?' or 'What is an altar?' And it is because simple questions like these have made Church people re-think fundamentals that we have some striking and successful new churches in our dioceses to-day.

So, too, before we revise the liturgical calendar we must ask questions. 'What is the calendar for?' and 'Is this Christian truth still expressed in this particular feast day?' We may conclude that the significance of an octave has vanished, or that Rogationtide is meaningless in an industrial society, or that an Ember Day is most profitably spent praying for more clergy. But whatever questions we ask, we shall find the most satisfying answers when we have achieved that delicate poise between respect for tradition and awareness of contemporary needs that is demonstrated architecturally in the finest of our modern churches.

The restoration of the great Fifty Days as a *laetissimum spatium* would not necessarily obliterate the festivals of Easter Day, Ascension Day and Whitsunday. It would frame them (as the events which they celebrate are framed in the New Testament) within the context of the living Church's faith in the new and wonderful harvest, in the presence of the Bridegroom, and in the law of the Spirit in unity and love.

So we would be led to contemplate the vision of our Lord

97

enthroned in the midst of his Church, and to be quickened afresh by the dynamic of the Holy Spirit in and through the people of God. Recalling the ancient themes and images associated with the great Fifty Days, the ministry of the Word would proclaim what we believe about God, about his world, and about his kingdom. And in response we would stand and rejoice, and take up the shout of praise:

ALLELUIA!

Appendix A—Lections for the Eucharist

The following table shows the readings from the Roman, Ambrosian, Spanish (Mozarabic) and Byzantine rites, together with the passages set in the Book of Common Prayer, for the Sundays and Ascension Day between Easter and Whitsun. The traditional association of St. John's Gospel, Acts and Revelation, noted on p. 64, can be traced in the various columns.

	BOOK OF COMMON PRAYER	ROMAN RITE	AMBROSIAN RITE	SPANISH RITE	BYZANTINE RITE
EASTER VIGIL		Col. 3:1-4 Matt. 28:1-7			
EASTER DAY	Col. 3:1-7 John 20:1-10	1 Cor. 5:7-8 Mark 16:1-7	Acts 1:1-8a 1 Cor. 15:3-10a John 20:11-18	Rev. 1:1-8 Acts 2:14-39 John 20:1-18	Acts 1:1-8 John 1:1-17
EASTER I	1 John 5:4-10 John 20:19-23	1 John 5:4-10 John 20:19-31	Acts 4:8-24a Col. 2:8-15 John 20:19-31	Rev. 5:1-13 Acts 13:26-39 John 20:19-31	Acts 5:12-20 John 20:19-31
EASTER II	1 Peter 2:19-25 John 10:11-16	1 Peter 2:21-5 John 10:11-16	Acts 9:19b-31 Phil. 3:17-21 John 1:29-34	Rev. 3:7-13 Acts 4:5-12 John 5:1-18	Acts 6:1-7 Mark 15:43-16:8
EASTER III	1 Peter 2:11-17 John 16:16-22	1 Peter 2:11-19 John 16:16-22	Acts 5:33-42 2 Cor. 7:10-13 John 16:16-22	Rev. 14:1-7 Acts 4:13-22 John 4:45-54	Acts 9:32-42 John 5:1-15
EASTER IV	James 1:17-21 John 16:5-15	James 1:17-21 John 16:5-14	Acts 4:32-5:11 Phil. 2:12-17 John 16:5-14	Rev. 19:11-16 Acts 4:23-31 Luke 8:41-9:2	Acts 11:19-30 John 4:5-42
EASTER V	James 1:22-7 John 16:23-33	James 1:22-7 John 16:23-30	Acts 9:32-42 Heb. 12:1b-7a John 16:23b-30	Rev. 22:1-5 Acts 5:12-32 Mark 2:13-22	Acts 16:16-34 John 9:1-38
ASCENSION DAY	Acts 1:1-11 Mark 16:14-20	Acts 1:1-11 Mark 16:14-20	Acts 1:8-14 Eph. 4:7-12 Luke 24:36-53	Rev. 4:1-11 Acts 1:1-11 John 16:5-22	Acts 1:1-12 Luke 24:36-53
SUNDAY AFTER ASCENSION	1 Peter 4:7-11 John 15:26-16:4	1 Peter 4:7-11a John 15:26-16:4	Acts 1:15-26 Rom. 3:19-26 John 17:1-26	Rev. 7:9-12 Acts 14:7-14 Mark 9:13-28	Acts 20:16-18a, 28-36 John 17:1-13
WHIT SUNDAY	Acts 2:1-11 John 14:15-31	Acts 2:1-11 John 14:23-31	Acts 2:1-11 1 Cor. 12:1-11 John 14:15-27a	Rev. 22:6-17 Acts 2:1-22 John 14:12-27	Acts 2:1-11 John 7:37-52 and 8:12

Appendix B—The Alternative Lectionary 1966

Since this book was written, the English Liturgical Commission of the Roman Catholic Church has published its *Alternative Lectionary* for experimental use in England and Wales. The lessons in this lectionary are intended to replace the readings at the weekday masses except on festivals and during Lent. In the period which we have been discussing, epistles and gospels are provided for all the weekdays except the Easter and Whitsun octaves, Ascension Day and its vigil.

The epistles are listed in two series, one for the first year and a second for the following year. In the first series the pericopes are taken from 1 Peter and Ephesians and in the second from Colossians and Hebrews. They are mainly concerned with the life of the faithful. The editors have given headings to the readings and looking down the columns one sees 'We must be holy as God is holy,' 'We have been chosen out to be saints,' 'May you live as God's servants,' 'Christ is our brother,' and so on.

There is, however, only one series of gospels, and these are all selected from St. John. From the Monday to the Saturday after Low Sunday the Bread of Heaven discourse from John 6 is read. During the week after Easter II the passages elaborate the theme of the Sunday's gospel, the Good Shepherd, from John 10. The remaining lessons are chosen from other parts of the fourth gospel which teach Christ's relationship with the Father and with his disciples. The reading of the High Priestly prayer in John 17, which begins on the vigil of the Ascension in the missal, is continued in the gospels for the Friday and the Saturday after that festival, while the lessons during the week before Whitsun tell of the promise and work of the Holy Spirit with verses from John 14, 15 and 16.

The *Alternative Lectionary*, then, is in no sense a revision of the calendar but simply an attempt to provide the Roman Catholic community with a consecutive series of Bible readings which can be used privately as well as during the liturgy throughout the year.

From what we have seen during the course of this book, the following comments might be made—though without implying any criticism, which would be unjustified here in the circumstances:

(1) Old Testament lessons are provided for all other weekdays in the year, but not during the great Fifty Days. Inasmuch as this lectionary recognizes the most joyful season, therefore, it does so by selecting readings entirely from the New Testament.

(2) The traditional policy of reading from the fourth gospel during the great Fifty Days is faithfully maintained. In general the passages are selected from those parts of our Lord's discourses which have a post-paschal implication.

(3) The tradition of reading the Acts of the Apostles has not been strengthened in any way. Passages from this book are already provided in the missal during the Easter and Whitsun octaves, but in the new lectionary the further lessons from Acts are set for the weekdays between Pentecost I (i.e. Trinity Sunday) and Pentecost V in the first series—clearly to continue the story of the apostolic Church after the commemoration of the gift of the Spirit on Whitsunday.

(4) The Book of Revelation, also traditionally associated with the great Fifty Days, is not read until the end of what Anglicans call Trinitytide (or during the weeks after Epiphany, if any of the Sundays have to be transferred).